Bridges:
How to Share a Witness across Worldview Barriers

Bridges: How to Share a Witness across Worldview Barriers
Copyright © 2012 Freddy Davis & Tal Davis

All rights reserved. This book is protected under the copyright laws of the United States of America. This book may not be copied or reprinted for commercial gain or profit. The use of short quotations or occasional page copying for personal or group study is permitted and encouraged. Permission will be granted upon request.

For Worldwide Distribution
Printed in USA

TSMPress
321 Anton Dr.
Tallahassee, FL 32312
850-383-9756

What People are Saying About this Book

Worldviews simplified!! This is the most understandable book about worldviews that I have read. The authors have provided a helpful resource that combines personal evangelism, apologetics, and interfaith equipping as well as making worldviews and working with persons of other worldviews more practical.
Robin Jumper, Ph.D., Dean of the Faculty
Professor of Evangelism and Missions
The Baptist College of Florida

In Bridges: How to Share a Witness Across Worldview Barriers, Freddy Davis and Tal Davis help us learn how to build a worldview bridge that will then allow construction of a Gospel bridge on which the Good News can travel more effectively.
James A. Smith Sr., Executive Editor
Florida Baptist Witness

This is a great book! I wish I had it recently teaching a class on Missions and Evangelism. I was very dissatisfied that all the resources I had on evangelism were the traditional way of presenting the gospel when that is just not what we encounter in society today. Cross-cultural missionaries are trained to understand religious worldviews and communicate the gospel in a context that can be received. We are having diminishing evangelistic success in our own country is due to our failure to recognize and understand differing worldviews in our own society. This book on bridging worldviews is a long overdue resource that will equip the reader for more effective sharing of the gospel.
Jerry Rankin, President Emeritus
International Mission Board. SBC

Freddy and Tal Davis' book, "*Bridges*," is a much-needed resource in a nation that is losing her way.
Dan Smithwick, President
Nehemiah Institute

This book gives comprehensive approaches in sharing the Gospel in this pluralistic world. If you are looking for an effective witnessing tool for sharing the gospel to other faith groups, you must have a copy of it.
    Aslam Masih, Church Mobilization
    North American Mission Board

In this crucial work, Tal Davis and Freddy Davis have done us an invaluable service by giving us a compelling process to relate to people who have totally different assumptions – many quite alien – about the nature of truth and reality.
    Rudy Gonzalez, Ph.D.
    Dean, Wm. R. Marshall Center for Theological Studies
    Southwestern Baptist Theological Seminary

Tal Davis and Freddy Davis have created a resource that is engaging, thought-provoking, and informative. If you're looking for a resource that will teach you how to relate better with those who do not share your faith, this book is for you!
    Michael R. Licona, Ph.D., Assistant Professor in Theology
    Houston Baptist University

What a great book from a great ministry! There is no better combination to teach that than an international missionary and a world-class apologist. That's what Freddy Davis and Tal Davis bring to the table in this important book, and the kingdom of God will advance because of it!
    Dr. John Avant, Senior Pastor
    First Baptist Church West Monroe, Louisiana

For decades American Christians have used cookie-cutter, rote-memorization witnessing tools. But old realities no longer dominate the American landscape. Freddy Davis and Tal Davis draw on their understanding of worldviews to show us the critical need to understand the worldview of our audience.
    Sean McMahon, Executive Director
    Florida Baptist Association

Freddy Davis and Tal Davis have done the church a much needed service by writing this helpful book. It gives all the essential information needed to share and defend the Christian faith in the twenty-first century.
Dr. Phil Fernandes, President
Institute of Biblical Defense

Today we live in a pluralistic United States of America. With the advent of instant communication, travel and globalized immigration, it is no longer possible to live in a vacuum of differing religious knowledge. For Christians it is important to recognize the differences between biblical Christianity and other faiths and respectfully show the Way of Christ without compromise. Dr. Tal Davis and Dr. Freddy Davis are uniquely gifted teachers and practitioners with a burden for equipping Christians to share the Message of Christ in love and authenticity. *Bridges: How to Share a Witness across Worldview Barriers* will help anyone reach that goal.
N. S. R. K. Ravi, Ph.D., Evangelism Response Center
North American Mission Board

The world is coming to America. *Bridges* answers the question of how to witness to a diverse nation.
Larry A. Powell, General Director Missions North America
National Association of Free Will Baptists

Freddy Davis and Tal Davis have written an engaging book on rethinking how to share a witness for Christ in the 21st century. Most Christians desire to share their faith effectively, but as we share we often come across barriers to witnessing that make it difficult to share effectively. We are answering questions that the lost are no longer asking. As a pastor desiring to lead his church to be more affective and as a Christian wishing to more effectively share, I find this book is a great help in understanding how to more effectively share about Christ.
Curtis D. Clark - Senior Pastor
Thomasville Road Baptist Church, Tallahassee, FL

A generation or more ago America looked a lot more like Jerusalem 2 than Acts 17; those hearing the gospel had more in common with it, like the Jewish audience in Acts 2. But increasingly America looks like Mars Hill in Acts 17, requiring not a different gospel, but a different approach to sharing the gospel. in Bridges you will learn how to be more effective in sharing the timeless good news in a timely manner for our times.

Alvin L. Reid, PhD
Professor of Evangelism and Student Ministry/Bailey Smith Chair of Evangelism
Southeastern Baptist Theological Seminary

Table of Contents

Introduction ix
Part I - Introduction to Christian Witness 1
   Chapter 1 - Starting with the Basics 2
   Chapter 2 - Why a Knowledge of Worldview
      is Important for Witness 10
   Chapter 3 - Overview of the Witnessing Process 24

Part II - The Due Diligence of Christian Witness 37
   Chapter 4 - The Starting Point for Witness 38
   Chapter 5 - The Art of Argument 58

Part III - The Practice of Christian Witness 75
   Chapter 6 - Sharing an Effective Witness Presentation .. 76
   Chapter 7 - Witnessing in Daily Life 97

Part IV - Resources for Effective Witness 103
   Witnessing Resource 1 104
      Overview of Various Belief Systems
   Witnessing Resource 2 183
      Breakdown of Popular Witnessing Methods
   Witnessing Resource 3 198
      The Seven Worldview Questions
   Witnessing Resource 4 199
      Witnessing Issues Related to Cross Cultural Missions

Small Group Discussion Guide 202
Teacher's Guide for Witness Training 205

Introduction

In the past, missionaries who worked in an overseas environment had to use more complex approaches to witnessing than the average Christian in America. Why? Because they had to cross a belief bridge that American Christians didn't have to cross. Unfortunately, in contemporary times, that has all changed.

So what, exactly, is different? The answer is, the makeup of the people who live in America has changed. Religiously, we are a much more diverse nation than we used to be. Consequently, it is now almost impossible to exclusively use the approach to witnessing that was traditionally used in America and truly be effective. It is now necessary to expand our skill set and take the approaches that overseas missionaries always had to use.

Even as recently as the 1960s, the vast majority of Americans operated from the foundation of a Christian worldview. That is, even those who were not saved or not active in church, still, for the most part, believed in the God of the Bible. Not so anymore. And there are several reasons for the change.

First, Naturalism has come to dominate every corner of the culture. Our educational institutions have a Naturalistic base and every child going through that system is taught curriculum based on Naturalistic presuppositions. This does not mean that all of the teachers are Naturalists, but the system itself oozes Naturalistic belief and the kids get it almost by osmosis. Virtually no mention of God is allowed, so atheistic beliefs become the default environment. Along with that, Naturalistic assumptions underlie what is taught in the natural sciences, social sciences, business, the arts and virtually every other subject area. Interestingly, this is also true regarding the teaching of religion – even in many Christian universities and seminaries.

But it is not just the educational institutions that are effected. The entertainment industry is also dominated by Naturalistic beliefs. The rampant immorality and anti-God themes that are prominently portrayed in the movies, on television, in music, and on the stage are simply artistic expressions of Naturalistic assumptions.

The news media is also dominated by Naturalistic belief. The liberal bias of the mainstream news media has been well documented, and the liberal mindset is based on Naturalistic presuppositions.

But Naturalism is not the only competitor to the Christian faith. Because of modern information and transportation technology, all the other worldview beliefs have flooded into American culture, as well. In addition, the massive numbers of immigrants who have come into the country have brought their religions with them. Many native-born Americans have converted to other religions, having been influenced through contact with adherents of these beliefs.

Yes, it used to be much easier to share a witness in America than it is now. And the reason is not that the message has changed. Rather, it is because the people we must deliver the message to have changed.

It used to be that one could simply open up the Four Spiritual Laws, or some other step-by-step witnessing tool, and begin reading it to a non-believer. The Four Spiritual Laws starts out, "God loves you and has a wonderful plan for your life." When the vast majority heard that message, they knew exactly what you were talking about. They understood that you were talking about the God of the Bible.

But now, what if you read that to a Naturalist? They don't believe God exists and would stop you right there.

What if you read it to an Animist? They believe in many gods. They would ask you which one you are talking about.

What if you read it to a Far Eastern Thought believer? They don't believe in any kind of personal God. These words would make no sense to them.

What if you read it to a non-Christian Theist? They believe in God, but in a different one. They would totally misunderstand what you were saying.

It used to be that to share the gospel, we only needed to build one bridge – the gospel bridge – in order to share with an individual how they could invite Christ into their life. But now we need to build a second bridge – a worldview bridge – so that the gospel message can even make sense. Every believer must now have missionary skills when it comes to witnessing.

The purpose of this book is to equip you with an understanding of witness that allows you to share your faith with anyone you come in contact with, regardless of their worldview background. Here you will learn to build both bridges.

This kind of knowledge is obviously valuable for those who plan to go to a different culture or religion as a career or short term missionary. But it is now necessary even for the average lay Christian who wants to be an effective witness on the job, in school, or in other places in society. It is our prayer that this foundation will give you the tools you need to be confident and faithful in your witness as you live your life out in the world.

Part I - Introduction to Christian Witness

Chapter 1 - Starting with the Basics
Chapter 2 - Why a Knowledge of Worldview is Important for Witness
Chapter 3 - Overview of the Witnessing Process

Chapter 1

Starting with the Basics

"I object!" cried the defense lawyer. "The prosecution is badgering the witness!"

If you ever watch a TV courtroom drama, you doubtless will hear that statement or something like it uttered. A person is on the stand to give testimony about something, usually a crime they saw happen or have knowledge about. Two lawyers will question him or her, one wishing to establish the testimony as true and the other trying to discredit it. The judge or jury must then decide whether or not the testimony is trustworthy. We call the person giving the testimony a witness.

What is Witness?

The word witness is used widely in various settings, secular as well as religious. For instance, a common place it is used is in a courtroom, as we saw in the illustration above. But our purpose here is to look at the word specifically in a Christian context. We are particularly interested in how it applies in our Christian faith.

The Christian's use of the word applies in two different forms. We need to understand both to truly get at how this plays out in our faith life.

The first form of the word is a noun. In this form, the word refers to a person, like the one in a courtroom, who has firsthand experience of an event. In our Christian context, if we know Christ, we have firsthand knowledge of what he has done in us. We have witnessed how he generated change in our lives and are in a position to tell other people what happened. We are, thus, witnesses in the noun sense.

The second form of the word is a verb. When we give a witness, we are sharing a firsthand account of something we personally saw, heard, or experienced. So, in our Christian experience, if we personally have a relationship with Christ and tell someone about this experience, we are witnessing to what we know.

Based on the two definitions above, obviously, a person who is a witness is actually nothing more than a messenger. And when we share a witness we are simply telling people what Christ has done in our lives based on our firsthand experience.

Witness: Event or Process?

The teaching methodologies for typical witness training programs encourage Christians to find a venue in which to share a gospel presentation, then go for the jugular to bring a person to a decision all in one fell swoop. Most of these methods teach students to use this "cold call" approach to share the gospel. That is, an individual goes to someone's home or meets a person on the street and engages them in a conversation which leads to a witness opportunity. Many times the people being witnessed to in these situations are total strangers. Other times they may be known, but there is no personal relationship which would make for a natural conversation about faith matters.

This is not meant to denigrate street evangelism or other cold call witnessing experiences. These kinds of opportunities do have their place. But that approach should be the exception rather than the rule for most Christians. The number of believers called and spiritually gifted in the area of cold call evangelism is actually relatively small. And to force the majority of believers to use that method is to push them away from sharing their faith altogether.

A cold call approach to witnessing closely parallels a sales person in the secular world. A relatively small number of people truly have the personality and skills to be effective in cold call sales. Those who do tend to be quite at ease in that role and can often make a lot of money. But most people are simply not comfortable, or effective, doing that kind of work.

Like sales people in the secular arena, the number of believers spiritually gifted in the area of cold call evangelism is actually relatively small. Those gifted in that area can have very effective ministries as they share Christ in that way. But to force the majority of believers to use that method is to push them away from sharing their faith.

To more fully characterize this cold call approach, what we generally see is that the end of a witnessing presentation also represents the end of any further opportunity to share. The reason is that the witnessing experience is seen as an event rather than as a process. When witness is viewed as an event, an individual typically either makes a decision to accept Christ or reject him right there on the spot at the conclusion of the gospel presentation. Whatever decision the one being witnessed to makes, there is typically no relationship foundation in place capable of taking the person further. When it is over, it is over.

While certain situations call for an event approach, most witness should be conceived of as a process which occurs in the context of a relationship. Statistics show that far and away, most people who ever come to know Christ do so by the influence of a friend or family member. These are people we have an opportunity to be around and engage over time. This kind of situation gives us ample opportunity to encourage them to consider a relationship with God. It also ends up being the more normal and natural way of sharing a witness under most circumstances.

Occasionally our witness opportunity will be an event. Again, it is not that this approach to sharing one's faith is bad or wrong. It is just that it is very limited. Generally we should think of witnessing as an expression of our life, rather than merely as an event in which to participate. As we engage relationships in the course of everyday life, some of the people we interact with are not yet Christians. In order to fulfill Christ's commission to share our faith, we must learn to cultivate those relationships. In that way, we gain people's trust and are able to share our faith with them in the normal flow of life.

As we consider our witness, though, it is important to grasp the full scope of the witnessing process. If we don't see this big picture, we will end up with some very serious problems. One of them could be that we end up allowing responsibility to rest on our shoulders which doesn't belong to us. A second problem that often emerges is that we take on guilt that doesn't belong to us based on decisions other people make.

Who Are the Ones Involved in a Witness?

As we consider our witness, it is important to know who all of the players are and where they fit in the process. There is more than one player in the game. In fact, there are three players and all have their own role to play. Each one can only do his or her own part and no one can do that of the others. The truth is, human beings are free-will creatures who must make their own decisions regarding how they will interact with God. The part each one plays is affected by the decisions they make regarding the witness.

God's Part of the Process

Human beings are incapable of affecting one part of the witnessing process. We are not in a position to change another persons life. When a person invites Christ into his or her life, God performs a miracle which actually creates within the individual something which did not exist before. Only God can do that part and he does it based on a decision he made regarding his purpose for mankind.

When a human being is born into this world, God performs the first direct miracle by giving physical life. The individual life did not exist before God put it specifically in the embryo that developed into a human person.

This miracle of physical life is marvelous enough in and of itself, but because of the Fall the body that we end up in is a corrupted vessel. The very human spirit that is the essence of our personhood is permeated with sin which inclines us to do acts in life which cause separation between ourselves and God.

This is the reason we need the gospel message in the first place. God wants to fix the brokenness. But the fix cannot be done strictly on the human nature we already have. It requires a completely new nature.

So, when a person recognizes his or her separation from God, repents from sin and asks forgiveness, God performs a second miracle. At that point, he creates a new nature in us – something that did not exist before – and literally makes us a new creature.

Because of this new nature, we receive a new element in our lives which is not corrupted by sin. This provides a place within us where God can actually dwell. With that, he attaches himself to our lives in a way that did not previously exist.

In the process, he literally adopts us into his family. Before he created this new nature in us, we were only a creation of God. When we entered the personal relationship with him by repentance and received his forgiveness, we became an actual child in his family.

Our Part of the Process

The actual change that takes place in a person's life at salvation can only be accomplished by God. But for some reason, he has chosen to use human beings as instruments in the change process. While believers are not the agents of change, we do have a significant role to play in God's plan. We are the messengers God has designated to deliver knowledge of the possibility of salvation. There is no particular reason why God needed to allow us to partner with him this way. But using believers as messengers is a part of his plan to reach the entirety of humanity with the message and more fully spread his glory throughout his creation.

Christian witness is the primary means by which God makes that confrontation. Of course, God is not limited to just one way of operating in people's lives. If human witnesses are not faithful in sharing the message, or there is no one within physical proximity of an individual that God wants to confront, he is not without recourse. He is able to sufficiently confront people via their consciences and by orchestrating circumstances to make them face their need.

That being said, his primary tool is the witness of believers. God has commissioned Christian individuals to understand the message of the cross and proclaim it to a world separated from him. His plan is to use us to engage other people in a way that creates free and open relationships which allow for a witness.

The essence of God's purpose for his entire creation involves relationship. He created mankind for the purpose of having a new class of being capable of relating to him personally and extending his glory. In creating this new being, he put in us the very personhood characteristics of himself. An essential element of that pertains to relationships. This characteristic makes it possible not only to personally relate to God, but to relate to other people, as well. This capability is the platform for our witness.

Of course, we must begin by doing our due diligence. This means that we must gain an understanding of worldview and learn how to share the gospel message. We can't get away from that necessity. But the platform to do the sharing is in the relationships we make. As we develop relationships based on trust, we put ourselves in a position to share the gospel message in a way easily understood and accepted by those who need to know Christ.

The Recipient's Part of the Process

God has his part to play in the process, and salvation cannot occur unless he creates the new nature within an individual. Believers also have their part to play as messengers who convey the message to those who do not yet know Christ.

But there is a third party who must also participate. That third party is the person who is still separated from God.

When God created mankind, he created us in his image. This means that we have the same personhood characteristics as God himself. One of the key elements of God's, and thus man's, personhood is the ability to make free-will decisions.

When it comes to the subject of personal relationships, this is an absolutely essential trait to understand. For a relationship to be an objective reality, it must be entered into freely. A forced relationship is no relationship at all.

Because God is sovereign and all powerful, it would certainly have been possible for him to have made mankind as a creature with no choice. He could have forced himself on us by making us love him. One can certainly enjoy operating a robot, but it is impossible to have a personal relationship with one.

Beyond that, if God had made mankind with no free-will, he could have enjoyed a certain kind of companionship with us – much like a person can enjoy companionship with a pet dog or cat. But something is missing in that kind of interaction. A pet cannot self-consciously love back. It can show affection, but cannot express self-conscious love.

God created mankind with the ability to actually love him by means of a personal, free-will decision – in the same way that he shows love to us. And it is only when that kind of love is expressed as a two-way relationship, that the purpose of God's creation is able to be fulfilled.

And this brings us back to the very purpose of the creation in the first place. God did it to provide for himself a being whom he could love and who could freely love him back. This new creation was also a means by which the glory of God could be extended into an entirely new arena.

In all of this, there is one more thing that must be confronted. If mankind really does have a free will, then it is also possible for an individual to make a decision not to enter into a relationship with God.

At this point, we come back to the topic of the recipient's responsibility. God has opened the door for a relationship, but we must individually walk through it. The responsibility for the decision is squarely on the shoulder of each person. When we make that decision, though, God performs the miracle of creating a new nature within us and adopts us into his family.

How It All Fits Together

So we have the three components of God's plan for the salvation of mankind. There is God's part, the believer's part and the non-believer's part. We looked at the three parts individually. Now let's see how they all fit together.

Everything begins with God's purpose. The very existence of mankind, had its origin in the mind of God. He didn't just randomly start creating things to see where it might lead. He started with a purpose.

The purpose in God's mind was to create a being with whom he could have an intimate personal relationship. But in order for this being to exist, there had to be a place for him to live. The Bible does not share *why* God created mankind to exist in the kind of physical body that we have. But in his own purposes, he decided that the nature of this creature would be physical. Consequently, a physical environment was also required.

So, God created the physical universe which is finely tuned to support life. He then created the earth as the specific place in the physical universe where a mortal creature could exist. Following that, he created human beings who were capable of a relationship with himself.

At first, there were no problems. The entire material order was created without sin and God enjoyed an unhindered relationship with Adam and Eve on earth.

But one day, they were tempted by Satan to sin and they fell for the ruse. At that point, sin entered the created order in a way which permeated the entire creation. The nature of mankind was also breached and humanity became unworthy to stand in the presence of God. The relationship was broken.

But God was determined not to be defeated by Satan and instituted a process which would lead to the redemption of his created order. For the redemption to take place, the penalty for sin had to be paid – and the penalty was death.

The death penalty should be paid by those who commit the sin. And indeed, it is designed to work that way. But God also provided a means whereby the penalty could be paid by someone else. But that someone had to be a person who had not been tainted by sin. Since no mortal human could qualify, God took it upon himself. He took the form of a human being, the man Jesus Christ, and lived a sinless life in order to qualify as the sacrifice for sin. He then paid the penalty for sin by his death on the cross. The resurrection of Christ was the confirmation that the power of God was up to the task.

While the death and resurrection of Christ is sufficient to accomplish the salvation of all human beings, God does not impose it on anyone. He offers it freely, but each individual must decide that he or she wants to receive it. At this point, we come face to face with the responsibility of the recipient. Every person who decides to ask God for forgiveness, and who gives his or her life to Him, is given the new nature and adopted into God's family.

But he did not leave it there. In order to spread the word about his offer of salvation, God commissioned believers to partner with him to tell the story. As members of God's family, we are given the privilege of working together with him to accomplish the purpose of bringing mankind into relationship with himself. With this, all three parts of the puzzle come together to fulfill God's plan.

Chapter 2

Why a Knowledge of Worldview is Important for Witness

Robert Bolt's award winning play and movie, *A Man for All Seasons*, tells the story of Sir Thomas More who, from 1478 - 1535, was the Chancellor of England. More was charged with treason because he would not sign a document validating King Henry VIII's divorce and remarriage. More refused to sign because he saw it as a violation of his Roman Catholic conscience.

In Bolt's script of More's trial, he uses a clever rhetorical illustration of how people's assumptions can be wrong. More asks the court to consider whether the earth is flat or round, a question still being debated in the 16th century. Assuming, he argued, that the earth is indeed flat, does it become round just because the King says it is round, and everyone believes it? Or, if it is indeed round but the King and everyone says it is flat, will that make it flat?

Virtually no one today would argue the "round earth" issue, but the principle remains. Many people today still assume certain ideas to be true because it is what they have been told or taught and have never had their beliefs challenged. This gets at the very essence of worldview.

What is Worldview?

As we begin to explore the entanglement of witness and worldview, it would be prudent to take a moment to explain what we mean by the term. We need to do this because we must know what we are dealing with before we can ever expect to grasp the implications of worldview in the witnessing process.

Interestingly, up until a couple of generations ago, this kind of knowledge was not an essential part of witness for most Americans. Since the vast majority in America used to operate from the same worldview foundation, a worldview bridge did not typically have to be built in order to share the gospel. It was possible to go directly to building the "gospel bridge." That simply is not the case anymore. Now, we need to also be able to deal with people's worldview foundation.

Everyone in the world, without exception, has a set of beliefs that form the foundation of their lives. While most Christians would probably assert that this foundational set of beliefs consists of their Christian faith, that would not be true. In dealing with worldview, we are speaking of a set of beliefs so basic that even the Christian faith does not make sense without them. Thus, it is fair to say that most people could not articulate their worldview beliefs even if directly asked to do so. Nonetheless, they have them anyway. Everyone lives by a set of assumptions concerning the nature of reality. And that concept forms the core of our definition of worldview. ***Worldview is the set of assumptions people make about the nature of reality.***

At first glance, this definition may seem a bit esoteric and philosophical. And perhaps it is. But the implications of the truth in this definition are actually quite clear and practical. In fact, it is fair to say that nothing is more practical in a person's life than coming to an understanding of their worldview. Everyone has a set of beliefs about how reality is structured, and everyone lives as if these beliefs are true – whether they are consciously aware of them or not.

There is a serious problem, though. There are several possible worldviews one may hold and every one of them literally contradicts every other one. That being the case, all of them cannot be true at the same time. In fact, it is only possible for one worldview in the entire world to be true. There is only one way that reality is actually structured, and the beliefs that match up with it are the only ones which correspond with that structure.

So, what is the end result? First, it means that the beliefs most people hold at a worldview level are not true. What we end up with, then, is a situation in which the majority of people in the world live life "as if" reality were structured in a certain way (the way they believe), even though it is not. This is important because it affects how they interact with every part of life (possessions, relationships, personal attitudes, government, morality, and so on), and it affects how they interact with the supernatural world (what they believe about God, heaven, hell, etc.). Looking at it this way, we can appreciate how our worldview beliefs affect our own life and witness, and why it is important to understand where non-believer's ideas come from.

In some ways this may seem strange because the way we understand how reality is structured seems so obvious. The problem is, though, the structure of reality is not something that can be analyzed empirically. No person can go into a lab and perform experiments to prove scientifically that what they believe at a worldview level is true. We can experience parts of life in the physical world by empirical means, but other parts have to be discerned by faith (Is there a God, or not? Is there a spiritual realm, or not? Does sin exist, or not?).

While the topic of worldview may seem a bit daunting at first glance, it is not nearly as difficult as it might appear. Let's take a moment to break down the definition and focus on the key words in order to grasp their significance.

The first key word we need to look at is *assumptions*. A worldview is a set of *assumptions* about the nature of reality. An assumption is nothing more than a belief that seems so obvious to a person that it is unimaginable that other people could see things differently. For instance, for a Christian it is hard to imagine that some people don't believe that God exists (even when they say they don't). And, for a Naturalist it is hard to fathom that Christians actually believe in the "superstition" that God does exist. Based on their worldview foundation, people hold beliefs that, to them, seem so obvious that they never even consider the possibility that it might not be true.

The second word we need to understand in this definition is *reality*. When we think of how all of existence is structured, we delve into the realm of "the nature of reality." The entirety of reality is structured in some actual way and is not structured in any other way. There either is a supernatural world or there is not. God either exists or he does not. It is certainly possible to imagine some non-actual ways that reality might be structured. But no matter how creatively it is described, it does not change the way things really are. This actual structure of the way things are is what we call reality. We can also refer to it as Truth (with a capital T). Truth, in its most fundamental form, relates to the set of beliefs that most closely lines up with how reality is actually structured.

Now that we have looked at the pieces, let's put it all together and see if we can grasp the full scope of the definition. Worldview is a faith position (set of assumptions) which is the organizing principle for an individual's understanding of how the real world is structured and how it operates (nature of reality). The possibility that the set of beliefs which someone holds may or may not correspond with the way reality is *actually* structured is quite beside the point. In fact, human beings are fully capable of living their lives from birth to death based on an understanding of reality that is not true. In fact, billions of people all over the world do just that.

And since we cannot physically see or measure the structure of reality itself, we are left to gather various other kinds of evidence to support our position. We have no choice but to select a position and to live by it (though most people don't actually select theirs, they just grow up in it).

This brings us to why we need to deal with the topic of worldview. As Christians, we believe that there is a real, personal God who created and sustains the material world and who has revealed himself in the Bible. A lot of evidence supports our claim, but we can bring no physical proof to the table to scientifically demonstrate our belief.

Of course, everyone else in the world is in the same boat. Some believe in a God that is different than the one revealed in the Bible, or that there is no God, or that there are many gods, or that the cosmos consists of an ultimate impersonal life force. These are some of the faith positions that are widely held by people throughout the world.

As Christians, we believe that what is revealed in the Bible represents actual reality. Anyone who believes something different lives by a set of faith presuppositions which comes from another place. We need to know why our faith position is the Truth and others are not. We also need to know how to share our faith with people who hold other assumptions. We can only do this if we grasp the full implications of the concept of worldview. Let's consider a couple of analogies to help us understand the nature of worldview beliefs.

In our first analogy, we will compare a person's worldview to the foundation of a building. Before the superstructure of a building is ever put up, the foundation has to be laid. There are two parts of this foundation that are critical. The first is its shape. When a foundation is laid, it defines the possible parameters of the building. One can make the building smaller than the foundation, but cannot build outside of it. The second critical part of the foundation is its strength. The superstructure can be made lighter than what the foundation can support, but not heavier.

A worldview is a belief foundation. First, it defines the structure of the belief system. Beliefs which go outside of the foundation belong to some other system, not to the one defined by the worldview. Secondly, the worldview beliefs must be strong enough to support the belief system. There cannot be contradictions, historical untruths or logical weaknesses or the belief system cannot stand.

In our second analogy, we will compare worldview to eye glasses. Living life based on a non-Christian worldview is much like looking through a pair of red glasses – it alters what you see. If you have looked through those red lenses all of your life, everything looks normal because that is all you know. If you happened to put on a pair of glasses with uncolored lenses, it would look abnormal – even though you would be seeing what actually exists. It is only when you come to the realization that the uncolored lenses show you actual reality, that you are able to fully appreciate what you are seeing. Until you come to that realization, you will live life "as if" the red tinted glasses represent reality and continue to believe that the clear ones actually skew it.

A person's worldview is a set of faith lenses. People look through their worldview beliefs to understand the world. If their worldview beliefs do not represent actual reality, they just don't know it and live on *as if* their beliefs were true – even though they are not. It will, certainly, skew many things as they must live in the real world, but they will simply not be aware of the inconsistencies that it brings on. It is possible for people to live their entire lives looking through a false set of beliefs and actually believe that their faith is the Truth. But it doesn't alter the fact that it is not.

Where a Worldview Comes From

If a worldview is a set of assumptions, these assumptions must come from somewhere. So just how do people come to a place in life where they personally affirm a particular set of beliefs?

Initially, a person's worldview emerges from the environment in which they were raised. When children are growing up, they don't have the perspective or the skills to analyze the things they are taught. They simply live in a household and accept, at face value, the things they hear from people they trust. A person's first beliefs are merely accepted based on the direct and indirect influences of the significant people in their lives.

In fact, as a child, individuals do not even realize that there are other perspectives than what they grew up with. And for many, this condition carries on throughout their entire lifetimes. Even though there are multiple worldviews, unless a person is somehow brought to a conscious awareness of other beliefs, or they make a deliberate effort to discover them, all they will ever know are those they were exposed to when they were young.

It is not unusual, though, for individuals to be confronted, at some point in life, with a different worldview. Since these different worldview beliefs literally contradict their own beliefs at the most fundamental level, this can often create a belief crisis.

This brings us to a second possible source for worldview beliefs – a collision of worldviews. Sometimes when a person confronts a new worldview, it creates an internal crisis which causes him or her to deeply question previous beliefs. If this crisis is compelling enough, it is quite possible that the individual would even change over to another set of beliefs. Typically when this happens, it results in a very dramatic and emotional experience. This often happens when a person converts from some other belief to faith in Christ. It is also what happens when a person converts from Christianity to some other belief.

There is a third way that a person can come to own a worldview belief system – by choice. It is possible for individuals to study the different worldview possibilities, then choose the one that seems to correspond most closely with the way they perceive reality. This is one of the main reasons we should make the effort to understand the concept of worldview. This not only helps us understand our own faith better, but also the default beliefs of those we wish to witness to. If we are going to ask people to switch worldviews, we need to know what we are asking them to do.

It might be noted that this third way tends to be the least used because most people never purposely become consciously aware of other worldview systems. Thus, they are not aware of the various possibilities and don't develop the ability to compare the options.

What Makes Witnessing so Difficult

Having alluded to the difficulty of changing worldviews, let's look a bit more deeply at why this is the case. This can not only help us be more compassionate toward the people we wish to witness to, but more patient with them as they consider the message, as well.

We need to recognize that change involves mental, physical, emotional and spiritual experience. When a person makes a change, all four of these need to be addressed. This is actually true for any change we try to make in our lives, not just those related to our religious beliefs.

First we must recognize the mental aspect of change. Every change is based on an understanding of something. Without this understanding, a person can't even know what they ought to change, much less how to generate the change. In our witness, we have to make sure the person we are witnessing to fully understands what we are asking them to change. Depending on the individual's starting point, this could be a very easy or a very difficult matter. If they grew up in a Christian, or even some kind of Theistic environment, the Christian faith may not be so difficult to grasp. If they grew up in some other worldview environment, however, the Christian message may seem very strange indeed, and may take them some time to understand.

Secondly, change has a physiological component. As humans, we are essentially spiritual beings, but are housed in a physical body. Our bodies operate based on physical laws, some of which are operative within our bodies. When we make a change, there are new neural patterns in our brain that must be formed, and sometimes a life change requires new physical habits which even affect our muscular and other bodily systems. Anyone who has ever tried to start a new exercise routine knows how difficult this physical change can be. If someone wants to receive Christ, we may have to be patient with them as they struggle to create new habits in their lives. Many times, the new habits of a Christian life may conflict with the habits of the old carnal life.

Change also has an emotional element. Human beings become emotionally attached to the status quo (some of this is actually physiological, as well). Change may require giving up something that we are emotionally attached to. Christ calls believers to holiness. But people who have been enjoying an unholy life may find themselves missing certain activities or the interaction with certain non-believer friends. We must be ready to help people work through this.

And finally, change has a spiritual dimension. Particularly when it comes to changing in order to follow Christ, Satan is doing all he can to attack spiritually and keep that from happening. When we share a witness, we must be prepared to help the person face a spiritual attack like they have never experienced before.

Simply put, every part of the change process is a struggle. And when we ask a person to receive Christ, we are asking them to make a massive change – in thinking and in lifestyle. In fact, we are asking them to actually change their very identity. People simply don't give this up easily. Thus, as a witness, we need to be prepared to be patient and helpful to those who are considering that decision.

The Importance of Worldview in Witness - The Worldview Bridge

The reason Christians witness is because God has commissioned us to do so, nothing more and nothing less. We are admonished in Matthew 28:18-20: *Then Jesus came to them and said, "All authority in heaven and on earth has been given to me. Therefore go and make disciples of all nations, baptizing them in the name of the Father and of the Son and of the Holy Spirit, and teaching them to obey everything I have commanded you. And surely I am with you always, to the very end of the age."* NIV

But God commissioned us to this task for a reason. It is because it lines up with his purpose for creating humanity. He created us for relationship with himself and as a means of spreading his glory throughout the entirety of his creation. But in the current state of existence, all people are separated from him due to the fact that we have a fallen nature because of sin. But in his great desire to bring all of humanity back into relationship with himself, God has called on Christians to partner with him to show non-believers how they can be reconciled to him. This call to share is what witnessing is all about.

Without a doubt, some obstacles to witnessing will be faced. One difficulty is the fear of sharing this message with certain people. Another is a lack of knowledge about the message we are called on to share. For some, there is even a problem because of certain lifestyle choices. But these obstacles are not valid excuses for putting aside God's stated will for our lives. Rather, we must overcome whatever difficulties we face in order to be faithful to God's calling on our lives. Fear is most often due to a lack of knowledge. We don't fear sharing what we are expert on. So, by equipping ourselves effectively concerning the elements of witness, we eliminate both the fear and the lack of knowledge. As with any lifestyle issue, doing this is simply a matter of making a decision to put aside sin and to live in fellowship with God.

A person's worldview is a powerful set of beliefs. It is the foundation of one's very identity. When you tamper with a person's worldview, you knock the legs out from under their understanding of reality. This is quite profound and can be tremendously unsettling. When we ask people give up their foundation and accept a new one in Christ, we are asking them to change their life's orientation. Virtually no one makes that change without significant inner wrestling. If we want to be effective witnesses, we need to know what other people believe and how to craft the message of Christ in a way that makes sense to them.

As we consider sharing a witness based on an understanding of worldview, let's take a look at some of the reasons this approach helps us.

Reason #1 - It Helps Us Understand Faith

One of the most important points to understand regarding the topic of worldview is that every worldview is built on a faith foundation. This can be a critical matter when it comes to the opportunity for witness.

Some worldview positions acknowledge this faith presupposition up front. In fact, this is actually one of the central elements in our

Christian faith. Christians assert that individuals must receive Christ by faith. But this does not mean there is no evidence for our belief. In fact, substantial evidence supports our Christian faith. It is just that there is no proof which can be brought forth to satisfy a totally empirical inquiry.

Honestly though, most non-Christians don't consider the faith foundation for their own beliefs. In fact, most don't even know it, or won't acknowledge it. For most, if their belief seems reasonable to them on a surface level, they just accept it without even considering where it came from. But, going back to our definition of a worldview, we see that it is a set of assumptions – a faith position. Still, most people never even consider the possibility of challenging the assumptions they follow. They simply believe them and that is good enough.

There are, though, those who honestly believe that their worldview dogma is solidly based on an empirical foundation. This is particularly true for those who adhere to Naturalism. After all, for them the material world is all that exists. They assume that everything, without exception, can be dealt with through experiment and observation if only the technology is available. Nonetheless, there are no empirical answers to the questions which define people's worldview beliefs, regardless of their foundation.

As such, one of the first things we need to do in our witness is to establish the person's faith foundation. By doing that, we are in a position to question the validity of their faith. The purpose for doing this is not to be vindictive. It is certainly possible to win the battle and lose the war. That is the last thing we would ever want to do.

But the fact is, most people who are anti-Christian are very practiced at throwing what they consider inconsistencies in our face. They attack us by questioning the validity of our faith. When people do this, it is important for us to get on an equal footing with them. By understanding the faith foundation of other worldview positions, we are able to bring questions into the minds of unbelievers about the validity of their faith. This, then, begins to pry an opening for our message to slip into.

Reason #2 - It Helps Us See the Objective Truth of the Gospel

The fact that the Christian worldview is based on a faith foundation does not mean that it does not represent objective reality.

Just because we cannot verify a particular belief system based purely on empirical data does not mean it is false.

The truth of the matter is, some worldview position does represent the way reality is actually structured. And whatever worldview belief that turns out to be, it is still a faith position. It cannot be otherwise, since no worldview can be verified purely on an empirical basis. That leaves us with the task of trying to discover what belief system does represent objective truth using logic and human experience along with the empirical evidence. As we examine carefully the Christian faith, the evidence strongly demonstrates that it truly is the objective truth about how reality exists.

Reason #3 - It Gives Us Confidence in the Truth of the Gospel

At this point we come to one of the most important aspects of how understanding worldview fits into the witnessing process. In a word, knowing that our belief is the truth about reality gives us confidence to share our faith with others.

Why is it, then, that such a large percentage of Christians are not willing to share their faith? There are two critical reasons.

First, most Christians do not have a working knowledge of the gospel message itself. If you don't know the content of the message, how are you going to share it? Simply put, you can't. Worldview training gives us the knowledge we need to confidently tell the message.

But there is another reason Christians tend be unwilling to share their faith. They are not completely sure that they can answer the objections of people who might oppose them.

But when we know that what we are sharing is the objective truth about reality, and why it is the truth, we no longer fear arguments people might throw our way. Our worldview training gives us this knowledge, as well.

No one wants to be in a vulnerable position when it comes to faith matters. If we don't know the content of the message or we don't understand why our faith is the truth and others are not, it is only natural that we would avoid discussing the topic. But if we take seriously our study of worldview, we have all of the knowledge necessary to stand up to any situation.

This confidence is especially important in a couple of settings. Perhaps the most obvious is when we engage people who are hostile to our faith. Not only do they come at us with a bad attitude, but they also hit us with the most difficult questions to answer. But when we truly understand worldview, we are not only able to deflect their attacks, we can even put them on the defensive.

Our need for confidence is not limited to those who are hostile, however. We need it even when we engage those who are quite interested in our message. Many of the honest questions people have can cause us great insecurity if we are not able to answer them. Often people are truly searching for the answers about the problem of evil, the question of suffering, the seeming injustice in the world and so on. Understanding worldview gives us a means for dealing with these questions, as well.

Once we have true confidence in our faith, there is no situation which will make us uncomfortable. At that point, we are capable of sharing a witness, come what may.

Reason #4 - It Provides an Understanding of the Beliefs of Others

We have dealt extensively with the importance of understanding worldview. It concretely helps us see the contrast between the truth and all of the false belief systems we encounter. We need this understanding for our own confidence, but it also gives us a powerful tool for explaining that truth to others. If we can show people why their worldview is not true, they are more likely to respond positively to our gospel presentation. This does not necessarily mean they will accept the Lord, but it may create an opening through which his Spirit can move.

The reason an understanding of worldview is so important for witnessing is because to be effective in sharing our faith, we must present the gospel in a way that makes sense to the one we are talking to.

For example, suppose you want to witness to someone who claims to be a Wiccan. We know that this is a form of Animism and that Animists do not recognize God as a transcendent individual person. They believe in many gods that are manifested in nature. They believe that by using the proper incantations, humans can manipulate their power.

If you begin sharing your faith with Wiccans as if they already understood God to be the person revealed in the Bible, they likely will not understand what you are talking about. They understand supernatural beings to be an entirely different class of creatures.

If you want your presentation to make sense to them, you must start at a different place. You must first explain who God is and what he is like. And you must do this until they finally understand what you mean. Even if they never come to the place of accepting Christ, you must still bring them to an understanding of the biblical God for it to even be possible. So, you have to begin by distinguishing the God of the Bible from the gods that they follow.

What is true for Animism is true for every other worldview belief system. The people you want to share with come to you with a set of religious beliefs already in place. You must discern what their starting place is and tailor your explanation to it.

The Christian plan of salvation assumes a certain knowledge of God. It is part of the core worldview beliefs a Christian holds. If the person you are sharing with does not have that initial knowledge, they will not understand your gospel presentation.

Every worldview has its own understanding of salvation. Each assumes a different starting point and outcome for salvation. We need to know each person's starting point and why it is wrong. Then, when we witness to someone with a different worldview, we must convey a certain amount of knowledge about why their view does not line up with reality. From that point, we can lay a foundation about the Christian understanding of salvation and present the gospel message meaningfully.

Reason #5 - It Provides an Understanding of the Weaknesses of Other Faiths

Wouldn't it be wonderful if all we needed to know was the positive message of the Christian plan of salvation? If that were the case, we would never have to be concerned with the beliefs of others. It would certainly simplify the task of sharing our Christian faith. And, indeed, that is the way it used to be.

Alas, such is not the case anymore. Every person we ever engage in witness comes to us with a worldview position already in place. If that position is based on a Christian worldview, our task is greatly simplified. Since that person already substantially agrees with us, we don't have to convince him or her of the truth of the Christian faith. All we need to do in that case is simply present the gospel message and offer the opportunity to respond to it.

But more and more, the people we engage come to us from entirely different worldview backgrounds. When that is the case, a completely different dynamic is at play. Not only do we have to share our own message, we have to overcome the message they already hold.

Generally when people attack our Christian faith, they argue that Christian beliefs are not true or reliable. Every one of these objections can be overcome, but this process can be never ending. No matter how good an answer you give, people can always come up with something else.

When people deal with you in this mode, they are simply not ready or willing to listen. They are just looking to throw you another curve ball. Don't even try to hit it! Go to bat from a different perspective. Rather than constantly trying to defend your position, simply give up for a short time and make them explain what they believe. When you shift the discussion this way, all of a sudden the burden is on the other person to defend his or her position. When you know the weaknesses of other people's belief systems, you position yourself to break down the false beliefs that their worldview is founded upon.

Once again, this does not necessarily mean that they will accept your faith. But until their foundation is knocked out from under them, they will not even be willing to look in another place for a new one. When we understand worldview, we know the weaknesses of the opposing positions that others hold.

Back to the Purpose

At this point we need to reiterate a very important principle. The purpose of worldview knowledge is not to destroy other people. It is easy enough to win an argument. But if you do it with a wrong attitude, the person you are sharing with will simply not listen to you. Our purpose in having worldview knowledge is to be able to effectively share the gospel message to the point that others can understand and accept it. We must have a right attitude and a loving spirit toward all those we engage.

Chapter 3

Overview of the Witnessing Process

"Good morning," said Tom, approaching a young student who was sitting on the steps eating his lunch. This was his chance to witness to a new student on campus.

My name's Tom. What's yours?" They shook hands.

"Raj," the man replied smiling. "I'm a new student from India."

"That's great. May I ask you a few questions?" Tom asked.

"Uh, okay. What about?"

Tom went straight to the point, "Do you believe in God?"

"Which god?" Raj asked in return.

"You know, God God." Tom said.

"I believe in all the gods."

Tom looked at Raj with a puzzled glare. "Well, how many gods are there?"

"I don't know. Millions I guess."

"Millions?" Tom tried another approach, "Well, do you believe in Jesus?"

"Who's he?"

Tom was stunned. Was Raj serious? Did he not know who Jesus was? "Don't you read the Bible?"

"Is that the university newspaper?"

"It's the book of God's Word!"

"Which god?"

"Look Raj, don't you want to be saved?" Tom pleaded.

Overview of the Witnessing Process

"From what? I'm fine. I'm just eating lunch." Raj was now getting a bit annoyed.

"Sin!" Tom spelled it out, "You know, S-I-N."

"S-I-N? Has something to do with Trigonometry, right?"

Tom tried again, "Don't you want to go to the New Heaven?"

Raj looked puzzled, "That's in Connecticut, right? Why would I want to go there?"

Tom finally gave up exasperated. "Thanks for talking to me."

"You're welcome," replied Raj, relieved to see Tom leaving at last.

Tom thought to himself, "That guy sure has strange ideas."

Raj thought to himself, "That guy sure asks strange questions."

Tom's motives were certainly right in wanting to share Christ with Raj. But he failed to realize that his method was ineffective for the situation. Raj, a Hindu from India with no prior exposure to Christianity, had no idea what Tom was talking about. Their communication was on totally different wavelengths. In this chapter we examine how to engage anyone, no matter what they believe, in order to introduce them to Christ in ways that will make sense whatever their situation.

Before getting specifically into the "how-to's" of sharing a witness, it is probably a good idea to get a big picture of what is involved. A basic checklist of the necessary skills will assure the pieces are in place for an effective witness, no matter the circumstances.

Our purpose is to list all the pieces to the puzzle. While there is generally a certain order to these pieces, this is not simply a step-by-step process. The truth is, different situations call for different approaches and even different skills. Witnessing to one person may require a different knowledge base and a different way of interacting than with another person. You will be ready no matter what the situation if you have a big picture of the elements involved in the process and prepare for them in advance.

1. Do Your Due Diligence

Doing your due diligence is the initial preparation stage for witnessing. At this point you get ready to move toward the opportunities when they open up. Doing your due diligence falls into two categories. Category one is the knowledge base. You need to know certain things in order to share an effective witness. The second category is more personal – develop a desire to witness in ways that are attractive to the person to whom you witness.

Master the Knowledge Base

The knowledge base for effective witness is composed of four basic elements. Two of these concepts are necessary because they contain the content of the gospel message. The other two elements position you to gauge where the other person is in his or her current understanding. You can then deliver the message in a way that makes sense to the listener. We will start with the elements related to the individual you are witnessing to, as they tend to be neglected in most witness training programs. We will then look at the two parts which deal with the gospel message, itself.

1. A Basic Understanding of Worldview

We have already thoroughly defined worldview and examined why it is critical for Christians to understand. As such, it is a necessary part of witness training.

A person's worldview is the bedrock basis for everything else they believe. In fact, every religion, cult and philosophy emerges from one of only four worldviews. Some Christians may immediately object and proclaim that their Christian faith is their most basic set of beliefs. But that objection is not accurate. In fact, one's Christian faith doesn't even make sense if the worldview beliefs don't support it. For instance, if a person's worldview says God doesn't exist, then belief in the God of the Bible is impossible.

Only in relatively recent times has this become an issue. In times past, the worldview foundation for almost all of Western Civilization (Europe and the Americas) was Christian Theism. Even people who didn't claim to be Christians still believed in the existence of God. It used to be that you could whip out the Four Spiritual Laws booklet, or some similar witnessing tool, and share an understandable witness to almost anyone in those regions. In our current day, however, if you start sharing Christ by saying, "God loves you and has a wonderful plan for your life," people are just as likely to retort that they don't believe in God, believe in many gods, believe in the impersonal life force, or believe in some other god than the Christian one. Telling them, "God loves you and has a wonderful plan for your life" simply doesn't work under those circumstances.

The reason for the change is that Naturalism, Animism, Far Eastern Thought and non-Christian Theism are now prominent in society in ways they were not in previous generations. This diversity of thought makes witnessing more of a challenge than it used to be. Understanding worldview is the key to dealing with this intellectual state of affairs. We must now build a worldview bridge in addition to a gospel bridge.

2. The Specific Belief Background of the Person with Whom You Want to Witness

A worldview is a broad based set of beliefs. But within every worldview are many specific belief systems. All of the belief systems within a particular worldview have the same basic understanding of God, man and salvation, but express those concepts in different ways.

Understanding an individual's worldview foundation is the starting point for witness, but it does not give us all of the specific details we need to proceed effectively. For that, we need more knowledge about the person's particular faith group. For instance, both Mormons and Jehovah's Witnesses base their beliefs on a Theistic worldview. That being said, their stated doctrines of God, man and salvation are quite different from each other and from historic Christianity. So, in order to witness effectively to one of those folks, you should have some knowledge of their beliefs on these critical topics to distinguish between their and our essential doctrines.

3. The Scope of the Christian Worldview

The scope of the Christian worldview involves sharing the big picture story of the Christian faith. It starts with an explanation of the God of the Bible and his purpose for the creation of man and the universe. It then explains mankind's Fall, life after the Fall, redemption, and eternity. This is the full story of the Christian worldview. Sharing this big picture helps people see the differences between the Christian understanding of reality and their own.

4. The Essentials of the Christian Faith

The essentials of any belief system define the boundaries which cannot be crossed and still remain within that system. In the Christian faith, the essentials represent the actual gospel message. It draws a clear line around true biblical faith and tells people what they must believe if they wish to become followers of Christ.

The essentials of any belief system answer the fundamental questions: Who is God? What is a human being? What is salvation and how does one achieve it? This is the message one gives when sharing Christ by means of The Four Spiritual Laws, The Roman Road or any other Christian witnessing method. This is the message we must share in order to bring a person to the point of deciding to accept Christ into their own lives or not.

This fourth step is the beginning and the end of the witness for most traditional witnessing methods. This is not necessarily a bad thing, so long as the person being witnessed to already believes in the God of the Bible. That person already possesses a Christian worldview foundation, affirms that the Christian faith is true, and believes what the Bible teaches about God, his purpose, and the need to accept Christ. The only thing left, in that case, is to actually make the decision to receive Christ. However, for those who don't start with those basic beliefs and assumptions, it is critical to identify their worldview, determine their specific belief system, and to explain to them the scope of the Christian worldview before sharing the gospel message.

Master Yourself

Another element of due diligence is to prepare your own life to be a faithful witness. Without this preparation, people will see you as insincere and hypocritical.

1. Acquire the Necessary Perspective

Our attitude about virtually everything depends upon our life perspective. This is definitely true as it relates to our willingness to share a witness. It is easy to witness when we are emotionally "up." But it becomes more difficult when we are fatigued or emotionally dissatisfied with our faith at any given moment.

Our natural tendency is to look at life from our own personal perspective. This has specific implications regarding our witness.

For instance, when things are going well with our faith, we tend to be willing to share it with other people. But, when things are not going right, because of wrong decisions we have made or even simple fatigue, we simply don't "feel" like doing it. And for most people, when they don't "feel" like it, they simply won't do it.

But God did not make life to revolve around us. He made it to revolve around himself. If we really want fulfillment in life, we have to start where God starts. This means having a perspective not focused on self. It means we must first evaluate how our perspective affects the work of God's kingdom, then take appropriate action.

As it relates to humanity, the starting place is God's love. He loves everyone and wants a relationship with each individual human being. The right perspective means that we are not going by how we feel, but on what God wants to accomplish through us in any particular situation.

2. Intentionality

The second issue is self-mastery of the way we approach our witness to individuals. We need to be intentional. That is, we need to define our witnessing approach in our minds, develop a proper methodology, and plan a strategy for each person we wish to share with.

The fact is, many people in the world don't know God's love. If those individuals don't turn to Christ, they are headed to an eternity separated from him. Therefore, God has commissioned believers as his instruments to accomplish his purpose. Since we have personally experienced his work in our lives, we are witnesses of the fact that he is able to change a person's life. It is up to us to share that good news with those who do not know him.

As we think about our part in the work of God, we must recognize that simple intellectual assent to our responsibility is not enough to generate action. Many Christians acknowledge that they ought to share Christ with others, but just never do it. We have to exert some energy if we want something to be accomplished. In the case of our witness, we have to take the initiative to interact with other people.

Certainly, some people are naturally outgoing and make friends easily. But being an extrovert is not a requirement for making friends. Even the most introverted people have some friends. Truthfully, most people actually tend more toward isolation. In modern American society, with the development of social media, this trend is becoming even stronger. But as Christians, we have to buck the trend of focusing inwardly.

The easiest way to do this is to open ourselves up and let people know us. It is not necessary to be an extrovert. We only have to be transparent. When people recognize that we are open to them, they will naturally connect with us.

Once we have personally made the determination to open ourselves to others, we must then identify specific people with whom we need to share a witness. We have to make an intentional effort to become friends with those God places in our path. We can't always just be in "waiting" mode. Some people will not move toward us until we move toward them. This doesn't mean we should attack them with the gospel. Rather, we should go out of our way to be a friend. Once we do that, the witnessing opportunity will emerge in due time.

There is one additional point that needs to be made. Not everyone you interact with is going to be attracted to you. And, anyway, it is impossible for any single individual to verbally witness to everyone. That is why God has placed Christians in so many different places. Everyone has their own circle of influence. If we are open to relationships, some people will be attracted to us and appropriate opportunities will come.

3. Spiritual Preparation

Spiritual preparation is how we put ourselves into a position to be a worthy witness. It is a fact that in this life we will never reach sinless perfection. We can, though, grow in our relationship with God and continually move closer to the goal. In order to do this, we must keep our personal relationship with God up to date. We need to spend personal time with him and conform our lifestyle to his ways. This discipline will address the problem of our feelings of moral inadequacy.

We must get this personal internal element to witnessing right or we will feel uncomfortable sharing our faith. The way we engage our personal relationship with God is the key to this internal preparation.

Of course, the work of salvation is, ultimately, not a work that we do. God is the only one who can change a person's life. But if we are going to effectively carry the message of God, we must also carry the character of God. The message and the character cannot be separated. Two things will happen if we do not live our lives based on God's character.

First, the person we are trying to share with will not take us seriously. We will be seen as hypocritical if we share a message which calls a person to holiness, yet are not living it out in our own lives.

Secondly, we will personally feel inadequate to share the message. Not only will the other person identify us as hypocrites, we will feel that way about ourselves. It is very difficult to personally share Christ with someone from a platform where we feel unworthy to do it.

We must remember that witnessing is all about God and his purposes, not about us. The point is not for us to set records regarding how many people we can bring to Christ. The purpose is for individuals to come into a personal relationship with God through Jesus Christ.

2. Make Contact and Develop a Relationship

The second key component of effective witnessing can be wrapped up in the word relationship. When it comes to such a deep and sensitive topic as one's faith, most people are not going to take a random conversation seriously with someone they don't fully trust. We need to develop relationships that involve mutual trust and respect. At that point, it becomes possible to talk about anything, even religious matters, without offense.

In fact, the inclination of most people is to see witnessing simply as an event in which to participate at a particular moment in time, rather than as an expression of a relationship. The tendency is to set up the witnessing opportunity, carry out the witness, then end it.

The problem is, if we operate from an event perspective, all we have are incidents that occur from time to time which we complete and are done with. This is largely an impersonal approach. And with the event over, we either have to just let it go or try to set up a new event. Either way, we have lost out. If the person doesn't accept Christ, he will want to avoid us from that moment on, or at least not talk about that topic in future conversations. If he does accept Christ, the event is still over and it is often difficult to follow up and help him in the growth process.

Instead of thinking of it in terms of an event, we should be thinking of our witness in the context of an ongoing relationship. This way, the talk about Christ is part of a larger picture. Sometimes we talk about God, but other times we chat about food or sports or the kids or whatever. When the talk about God ends, we will have plenty more opportunities later on to address the issue. The relationship and the conversations continue. Then, if at some point the individual invites Christ into his life, we are able to continue to walk with him in a spiritual growth process which is actually a part of the relationship.

God literally has in mind those he wants us to share a witness with – and they are generally not just random individuals. Unfortunately, most witness training in modern times is taught in ways that promote this kind of randomness. We are taught a witnessing method and told to just go out and use it on people. That is not a bad thing per se, but it is not going to be particularly effective under most circumstances.

So, what do we do to keep our witness from being a random event? We insert intentionality into the process. This does not mean we can never share a witness on a spur-of-the-moment basis. There are certainly times when it is appropriate to do that. But statistics show the huge majority of people who come to know the Lord are influenced by someone they know well – like a close friend or relative. That being the case, it only makes sense to develop our witnessing strategy in this direction.

In order to continually have opportunities to share our faith, we need to consider in advance who we want to share our faith with. Having that in mind will inject us into the lives of those people and establish relationships which can lead to witness opportunities. This does not mean we will necessarily become best friends with every person with whom we interact. But without some kind of relationship, another person is generally not going to open up to us on the topic of their faith.

Our preparation for witness not only includes our preparation to deliver the message, but also of the people we want to interact with. We can begin, even now, to consider how we can be intentional with those we plan to engage.

3. Gather the Person's Worldview Information

A person's worldview relates to their most deeply held beliefs. Most people will not open up on that level unless we develop trust relationships with them. That is why it is so essential to make the development of relationships a priority.

As it turns out, many, if not most, people we know already hold our same basic worldview beliefs. We have a tendency to live around and interact with people who share the same basic backgrounds as ourselves.

But, typically, there are those who do not share our background, especially in our modern pluralistic society. More people than ever from different cultures, religions and philosophical backgrounds make up modern society.

So to share a witness, we not only need to know the specific beliefs of those who share our own worldview, but all of the others, as well. Even if we know how to give an effective gospel presentation but don't know where another person is coming from on a worldview level, our listeners may not fully understand what we are talking about. When we deal with people from other worldviews, we must figure out the right starting point for witness. This means knowing their worldview beliefs. So when we identify a person with whom we wish to share a witness, we must ask the kinds of questions which elicit information about their worldview background.

4. Analyze and Map the Worldview of the Individual

Once we find out a person's worldview foundation, we can analyze and understand it so that we can interact with that individual intelligently. It is pointless to begin sharing the gospel message with someone if they do not know who Christ is or do not believe he was God in the flesh.

The reason for analyzing a person's worldview is so that we can know where to start our witness. This starting point is critical. We can't assume our friend already understands who God is and what he is like.

For instance, if we start talking about the God of the Bible to a Buddhist, he is not going to fully comprehend that we are talking about a being who is personal and loving. Buddhists don't believe in a personal, loving God, and that kind of explanation will not make any sense to them. We will have to go back and give an explanation of the nature and character of God before we can share how to know him.

Everyone comes to us already having some understanding about the nature of reality. We must have some connecting point if we want our witness to make sense. We are then able to make explanations which they can understand.

Who is God?
As we have already seen, every belief system has some understanding about God – he doesn't exist, there are many, there is an impersonal life force, some non-Christian God, etc. Mapping a person's understanding of God simply means finding out specifically what they believe about him.

What is a Human Being?
Mapping this second question is simply to discover what the person believes about the nature of humanity. Are humans purely animals with a highly evolved brain? Are human beings spirit creatures in material bodies which symbiotically interact with the many gods which exist in the spirit world? Are we merely illusory expressions of the impersonal life force? Are we beings created by God for some purpose? If so, what God and for what purpose? It is essential to grasp this knowledge as a person's perceived understanding of the nature of humanity determines what he or she believes is necessary for salvation.

What Is Salvation and How Does One Achieve It?
Remember, salvation, in worldview terms, relates to the ultimate a person can get out of life – and every belief system has its own idea as to what that is. We map this by simply finding out from the individual what salvation is to them. As Christian witnesses, our purpose is to help nonbelievers understand Christian salvation, then build a bridge from their current beliefs to our Christian ones. We, thus, need to know what they believe so we can bridge the gap.

5. Understand the Commitment Level of the Individual
The level of commitment that people have regarding their faith is another very important factor to consider as we begin sharing our

faith with them. Their commitment level makes them either more or less willing to listen to what we have to say.

Many people we interact with do not have a high level of personal commitment to their faith. It is more of a cultural identity issue with them. People who are not highly committed will generally be more willing to listen to what we have to say. Their religious faith is not the primary driving force of their lives. This does not mean they are ready immediately to change. Even if their faith is just a cultural identity, it is still strong. Changing will still mean that they must reorient their lives. That being said, less committed people will generally be more ready to listen to our ideas if they are presented in a winsome way.

Others, though, are very much involved in and committed to their faith. These are people who recognize that their faith is the arena where personal strength comes from. They have probably engaged in a deeper level of training and involvement in their own faith. As such, it is necessary to make a heavier investment in a relationship with this kind of person in order to even get a hearing. The higher the commitment level, the stronger the case we will have to make.

It is important to understand this concept up front. We need to recognize that engaging relationships this way is generally not a quick and easy matter. It involves a long term strategy and requires a deeper commitment to the relationship. This commitment cannot be dependent on the outcome of our witness. We have to love them no matter what kind of decision they make in the short term.

Process Summary

Once again, the steps above do not necessarily represent a particular sequence in the witnessing process. Generally speaking, a certain order is represented, but every person we encounter tends to be at a different place in his or her understanding of and receptivity to a witness. We have to discern from our interaction with the individual what relationship elements need to be developed to share an effective witness.

That being said, these elements do represent the things we need to master in order to be a competent and effective witness. If we master these elements then make sharing a witness a priority in life, God will use us in powerful ways to bring people into relationship with himself.

Part II - The Due Diligence of Christian Witness

Chapter 4 - The Starting Point for Witness
Chapter 5 - The Art of Argument

Chapter 4

The Starting Point for Witness

"Sir," asked Wendy as she approached the man sitting at the lunch counter. "Are you familiar with the Roman Road?"

"Roman Road? No, I've never even been to Italy," he responded, a bit taken aback by her forwardness. "Why do ask?"

"Well, it's the way to get saved from your sins and go to heaven."

He winced and said, "Oh, but I'm not Catholic and don't know much about that church. In fact, I'm Jewish but I don't attend synagogue very often."

"I don't mean that Roman road, I'm not Catholic either. I'm talking about what it says in the book of Romans in the Bible."

"Which Bible? Yours or mine?"

"There's a difference?" she asked.

"Yes, we Jews don't accept what you call the New Testament as Scripture. Only the books of what you call the Old Testament."

Wendy did not know what else to say. She looked at the man, thanked him, and walked away.

Most people who are active witnesses use some kind of method for sharing Christ. Training programs which have been developed over the years include the Roman Road, The Four Spiritual Laws, FAITH, Steps to Peace with God, Evangelism Explosion, and many others.

Nothing is wrong with any method as long as it contains the essential points regarding how a person may receive Christ. But there are often problems leading up to the gospel presentation. Many methodologies start with a leading question. Here are some examples of the questions used by various systems.

- Have you ever heard of the Four Spiritual Laws?
- If you were to get to the gates of heaven and God were to ask why he should let you in, what would you say?
- If you were to die today, do you think you would go to heaven?
- Have you ever come to a point in your life where you trusted Jesus Christ as your personal Savior and Lord?
- How do you think someone becomes a Christian?
- In your personal opinion, what do you understand it takes for a person to go to heaven?
- Do you know for sure that you are going to be in heaven with God?

If you look carefully, you will notice a common denominator with all of these questions. All assume that the person being addressed has a Theistic worldview (believes in a transcendent God) – and many specifically assume the person has a Christian Theistic worldview (believes in the God of the Bible). They also presuppose a spiritual world exists that can be known and which people can enter at physical death.

If the person you witness to actually already holds a Theistic worldview, then these questions will probably at least be understandable. But what if the person doesn't believe that a supernatural reality even exists? What if this person believes in many gods who express themselves in nature? What if he or she believes that ultimate reality is an impersonal life force? What if the individual believes in a god, but not the one described in the Bible? What if that person contends it doesn't really matter what anyone believes? In any of these cases, the kinds of questions posed above will not be good places to start a witness. And today, an ever increasing number of people in America fit into those categories.

Bridge Building from One Worldview to Another

Different worldviews are so fundamentally dissimilar from one another that it is difficult for people from one worldview to understand or communicate effectively with those from another on topics related to faith. This is because people often have entirely different conceptions of the very structure of reality. This problem is demonstrated outwardly in life as people try to communicate with one another.

Typically, people with one worldview are not even aware of the depth of the divide between themselves and those who believe other worldviews. That is because we all use pretty much the same vocabulary. However, the nuances of the words we use are often very different. For instance, both Theists and Naturalists use the same word "morality," but the practical implications of that word are entirely different based on the presuppositions of the two worldviews. It is literally like speaking different languages without realizing you are doing so. What is true for the word morality is also true for such concepts as God, man, salvation, meaning, and the list goes on.

Building a bridge is an educational process. Even if people with different worldviews don't agree with each other, at least they need to understand what the other person believes if there is going to be valid communication.

As Christians, we want to share the gospel clearly with those who are not believers. But the gospel message assumes not only a Theistic worldview foundation, it also assumes Christian Theistic beliefs. If a person we are trying to witness to does not understand our Christian foundation, we must build a bridge for their understanding.

In actual fact, two bridges may be needed depending on the starting point of the person we wish to witness to. The first is a worldview bridge, if the person comes from a different worldview foundation. The second bridge is a gospel bridge which is able to share with them an understanding of our Christian faith.

Worldview Bridge

For those who come from a non-theistic worldview foundation, the first bridge built must be a worldview bridge. We must help them understand that there exists an actual transcendent God who is the Creator and Sustainer of the material universe. Their default belief will be something other than that.

We first have to explain to them what their own worldview foundation looks like. They likely have never consciously thought about it before. Remember, a worldview is a set of assumptions – mostly unconscious beliefs.

Following our explanation of their foundation, we must explain what our foundation looks like. With that accomplished, it becomes possible to compare and contrast the two. This last step establishes a basis for communicating the Christian worldview message in terms that make sense to the listener.

The truth is, every witnessing situation is unique. Everyone we witness to already has a worldview foundation that defines the boundaries of their beliefs. In order to share an effective witness, we have to create a bridge from what the other person believes to what we believe. This does not necessarily mean that person is going to accept Christ, but he or she will not even understand our message if we don't bridge the gap.

In order to figure out how to make this bridge, we need to create a belief map. A belief map is nothing more than an analysis of the essential beliefs of the person we wish to witness to.

Every belief system has certain doctrines which absolutely cannot be violated. They are so basic that changing even one of them actually moves a person into a different belief system. Adherents of any given system can and will disagree about non-essential beliefs. But they absolutely cannot disagree on the essential ones. We can get at these essential beliefs by asking three simple questions:

- What is the nature of ultimate reality? (What do you believe about God?)
- What is the nature of a human being?
- What is salvation and how is it achieved? (Salvation, in worldview terms, relates to the ultimate that the belief system has to offer.)

Every person within any given belief system will answer those questions the same way.

Gospel Bridge

Once the worldview gap is crossed, it becomes necessary to build another bridge – this one specifically for understanding the Christian faith. It might be noted, if the person already holds a non-Christian Theistic belief (Mormon, Jehovah's Witness, Jew, Muslim, etc.), building a worldview bridge is not generally necessary. You can usually begin immediately with the belief system portion.

Building the belief system bridge in the witnessing process begins with a systematic overview of the Christian faith. (This is dealt with more specifically in Chapter 6.) Essentially, we have to tell the Christian story. This begins with an explanation of God's purpose in creation, then moves on to the Fall, the results of the Fall, redemption, and eternity. Once people grasp this big picture narrative, they are in a position to understand the gospel message, itself. We also will deal with this topic in a later chapter.

Starting Point for the Basic Worldviews

When we wish to share a witness, we must begin by understanding the worldview foundation a person comes from. That is because each worldview has its own issues which we must address as we attempt to share Christ. Let's look at the major worldview categories to see the big picture issues that we need to be aware of.

Naturalism

1) Basic Assumption: There is no supernatural existence. The only thing that exists is matter which is eternal and evolving.

2) Major Belief Systems within the Naturalistic Worldview:
- Secular Humanism
- Atheism
- Agnosticism
- Skepticism
- Existentialism
- Marxism
- Positivism
- Postmodernism

3) Naturalism's Answers to the Essential Questions:
- What is the nature of ultimate reality? - There is no supernatural existence. All of reality is expressed within the natural universe.
- What is the nature of a human being? - Human beings are merely animal creatures which have a highly evolved brain.
- What is salvation and how is it achieved? - The ultimate life has

to offer is personal fulfillment. A person achieves this by doing whatever they find necessary based on personal goals and life dreams.

4) Weakness of Naturalism

In analyzing Naturalistic belief systems, we see that they all look to human reason as their authority source. They believe unaided human reason can lead to a definitive understanding of objective reality. The problem which emerges, though, is that Naturalism is, itself, a faith position lacking objective support. It is impossible to prove the foundational assumptions of this worldview. No one is able to empirically demonstrate that:

- matter has a natural source,
- life can emerge out of non-life,
- one life form can evolve into another, much less a more complex one, or
- consciousness can emerge out of non-consciousness.

All of these beliefs are foundational for Naturalism, and all of them are faith assumptions. This fact presents a huge problem for adherents of this position because they depend on faith assumptions to assert things they claim have an empirical base.

5) Starting Point for Witness to Naturalists

Naturalists believe they can arrive at Truth and come to a definitive understanding of objective reality by using unaided human reason. From that starting point, therefore, we must build a bridge to belief in the God of the Bible. In order to do that we must help them understand the following two worldview and three belief system bridge elements:

a. *Worldview Bridge Element #1: Naturalism itself is a faith position which completely lacks objective support.*

The bridge that must be created between Naturalism and Theism is the bridge leading from a belief in no God to one which asserts the existence of God. Building that bridge begins with helping an individual understand that his own belief that God does not exist is, itself, a faith position. Most Naturalists are unable to see this until it is pointed out to them.

We can demonstrate that it is impossible to prove empirically the foundational assumptions of Naturalism. No one is able, by observation and experience, to demonstrate that matter has a natural source, that life can emerge out of non-life, that one species can evolve in a way which takes it to another (much less a more complex one), or that consciousness can emerge out of non-consciousness. All of these presuppositions are foundational for Naturalism, and all of them are faith assumptions.

b. *Worldview Bridge #2: God is an objective person.*

The second part of the bridge in helping a person make the mental leap from Naturalism to Theism involves an explanation of the God of the Christian worldview. Since Naturalists don't believe in God (or any form of supernatural existence), they will not want to acknowledge even the possibility that God could exist. However, after recognizing that their own position is based on faith assumptions, they must at least acknowledge the possibility of a supernatural source for the existence of matter, life, complex creatures and consciousness, even if it is begrudgingly.

Of course, this does not mean they will immediately believe that the existence of God is true. But they must at least acknowledge that without evidence to the contrary, one faith position cannot trump another. So, even if they don't believe your explanation about God, they ought to at least be willing to listen to you and understand where you are coming from. Here, you are basically providing an alternative explanation for the source of the faith assumptions being made about the nature of reality.

c. *Belief System Bridge #1: The truth about God can only be known from the Bible.*

The validity of the authority source for the Christian faith is the first issue to address when specifically trying to bring a Naturalist to Christ. Some people may be willing to simply accept your assertion that the Bible is true. Others, however, will need you to demonstrate to them why the Bible is true. At this point, you will need to be conversant with evidence for the validity of the Bible. Numerous lines of evidence support the validity of the Christian authority source. As you share your witness, you may have to go into the reasons why the Bible is the Truth. If so, it is possible to go down that road and present very profound evidence.

Again, coming to an understanding of the Christian belief system does not mean that a Naturalist is going to agree with you about the existence of God. It is, though, a necessary step in the process.

d. *Belief System Bridge #2: Explain the Christian Worldview*

When an individual comes to the place where they grasp that the Bible is the authority source for the Christian belief system, it is then necessary to give an overview of the Christian faith. This begins with an explanation of God's purpose in creation, then moves on to deal with the Fall, the results of the fall, redemption, and eternity.

e. *Belief System Bridge #3: Explain the Gospel Message*

Once the person understands the big picture of the Christian faith, it is then possible to share the gospel message in a way that brings him or her to a decision point.

Animism

1) Basic Assumption: The universe contains both material and immaterial parts. Spirits exist in a separate place from physical beings, but they interact in a symbiotic relationship. Humans on earth offer sacrifices and perform rituals which benefit the spirits, and they, in turn, take care of the needs of humans on earth.

2) Major Belief Systems Within the Animistic Worldview:
- Japanese Shinto
- Voodoo/Santeria
- Wicca
- Native American Religions
- Astrology
- Fortunetelling
- Spiritism

3) Animism's Answers to the Essential Questions:
- What is the nature of ultimate reality? - There are many gods which exist in the spirit world who interact symbiotically with human beings in the physical world.

- What is the nature of a human being? - Human beings are spirit beings housed in a physical body. The human's spirit enters the spirit world at physical death.
- What is salvation and how is it achieved? - The ultimate aim is to live physical life without oppression. This is accomplished by living in harmony with the gods.

4) Weakness of Animism

Animists look to history and tradition as the authority source to back up their worldview assumptions. They believe the teachings about the nature of reality, passed down through multiple generations, is enough evidence to prove their worldview. Because of their presuppositions, they see the outworking of the god's actions in nature and don't recognize a need to look to revelation or science. However, their position has nothing to support it.

The fact is, many different Animistic traditions exist in the world. Any particular system is only one among many. Some of these different belief systems literally contradict one another on key points. That being the case, they cannot all be true.

The question then becomes: How is it possible to arbitrate between the different beliefs? How can one group know that their beliefs are true and others are false? The truth is, there is no way to do that. All that can be mustered is anecdotal evidence which, itself, depends on faith presuppositions. Something is not true simply because someone believes it.

5) Starting Point for Witness to Animists

Animists look primarily to tradition to support their worldview assumptions. They believe teachings about the nature of reality as passed down through the generations are enough of an authority. They see the outworking of the gods in the structure of nature and don't acknowledge any need for a sacred book or empirical science. Therefore, in order to effectively witness to an Animist, we must lead them to understand the following two worldview and the three belief system bridge elements:

The Starting Point for Witness

a. *Worldview Bridge #1 - The Animistic position has nothing to support it.*

As was mentioned above, many different Animistic traditions exist in the world. Any particular system is only one among many. This presents a serious problem because the different belief systems often contradict one another on key points. Therefore, they cannot all be true. Some of them must be wrong. That being the case, there must be some way of arbitrating between the different ones. But there is no way to make this determination. It is a faith position with nothing more than anecdotal evidence to back it up – and even then the evidence all depends on the faith assumptions of the worldview itself. So how can they know that their position is true and the others are false?

The specific matters you must use to deal with this issue are educational. At some point it will be necessary to teach the Animist another way to understand reality. When you do that, you can compare and contrast the two worldview systems side-by-side.

b. *Worldview Bridge #2 - There is only one God.*

Typically, Animistic belief systems hold that there are many gods. After getting a person to acknowledge the possibility that his belief could be wrong, it becomes possible to present an alternative. Since Christianity believes in only one God, it is necessary, at this point, to introduce him to this concept.

Essentially, we must explain the nature of the Christian God. We must tell the person what God is like and how it is possible that one God can account for all that exists. This explanation does not guarantee that the person will believe and accept the Christian faith. But unless he understands its content and acknowledges it as a possibility, you cannot bring him to any kind of decision.

c. *Belief System Bridge #1 - The truth about God can only be known from the Bible.*

Once a person understands that his belief system has no foundation and grasps the concept of a Theistic worldview, you are in a position to share the source of your own faith. At this point, explain how the Bible is the authority source of the Christian faith and share evidence to back it up

To do this, you will need to be conversant with the many lines of evidence which back up the Christian authority source. As you share your witness, you may have to go into the reasons why the Bible is the Truth.

Again, coming to an understanding of the Christian belief system does not guarantee that an Animist is going to agree with you about the nature of God. It is, though, a necessary step in the process.

d. *Belief System Bridge #2: Explain the Christian Worldview*
Once an individual recognizes the Bible as the authority source for the Christian belief system, it then becomes necessary to give an overview of the Christian faith. This begins with an explanation of God's purpose in creation, then moves on to deal with the Fall, the results of the Fall, redemption, and eternity.

e. *Belief System Bridge #3: Explain the Gospel Message*
Once the person understands the big picture of the Christian faith, you can share the gospel message in a way that brings him or her to a decision point.

Far Eastern Thought (FET)
1) Basic Assumption: In Far Eastern Thought, the essence of all existence is the impersonal life force. Pieces of that life force have spun off from the central core, but are constantly working their way back with the ultimate goal to re-merge with it. All of life in the physical universe is nothing more than pieces of that life force working their way toward reunification with the main body through successive material incarnations. The lower the life form, the further it has to go. To progress forward in this process, the life form, at whatever stage in the reincarnation cycle, must live its life in such a way as to accumulate good karma. If it does well, it will move up to a higher form in its next incarnation. When it makes it to the highest level and does well, the material reincarnations cease and the life force merges with the impersonal main body. The essence of this worldview is pantheistic and monistic.

2) Major Belief Systems Within the FET Worldview:
- Hinduism
- Buddhism
- Krishna
- Transcendental Meditation
- Jainism
- Sikhism

3) FET's Answers to the Essential Questions:
- What is the nature of ultimate reality? - Ultimate reality is an impersonal life force. Everything, in all of existence, is made up of some expression of this life force.
- What is the nature of a human being? - Human beings are one expression of the impersonal life force which has spun away from the main body. Humans are at a particular stage in the cycles of reincarnation which seems to be self-conscious and personal. This, however, is an illusion since the life force is impersonal.
- What is salvation and how is it achieved? - Salvation, in FET, occurs when the pieces of the life force which have spun off of the main body, are able to reunite with it. This is accomplished as the life force reincarnates over many lifetimes to higher and higher levels until it reaches the jumping off point. For human beings, the ultimate goal is to live the current life in such a way as to accumulate good karma. This allows the life force to advance to a higher level in its next life.

4) Weakness of FET

Adherents of Far Eastern Thought look primarily to human experience to validate their worldview assumptions. They take the beliefs which have been passed down through the ages and filter them through personal experience.

Once again, we have a situation where there is nothing to support the belief system. In fact, Far Eastern Thought has the same essential problem as was seen in Animism. In this case, however, the problem area is human experience rather than tradition. People from many different belief systems experience reality in contradictory ways. Unfortunately, no authority can arbitrate between the contradictory experiences of the different systems. Something is not true simply because someone has a certain kind of experience.

5) Starting Point for Witness to FET Believers

Adherents of Far Eastern Thought look primarily to human experience to validate their worldview assumptions. Essentially, they take the beliefs which have been passed down through the ages and filter them through their personal experience for validation. Therefore, in order to effectively witness to an adherent of Far Eastern Thought, we must understand their base assumptions and begin the witness there.

a. *Worldview Bridge #1 - The Far Eastern Thought position has nothing to support it.*

The Far Eastern Thought position uses human experience as its ultimate authority source. However, people from many different belief systems experience reality in contradictory ways. The question becomes: Who is able to arbitrate between the contradictory experiences of the different belief systems? Something is not true simply because someone has a certain kind of experience. Truth is an objective reality which can possibly be confirmed in some ways by experience, but not proven by it.

The specific matters one must deal with regarding this issue are educational. At some point it will be necessary to teach the Far Eastern Thought believer that there is another way to understand reality. When you do that, you can put the two worldview systems side-by-side and make the comparison.

b. *Worldview Bridge #2 - God is a personal, objective person.*

Once a person is brought to the place where he or she is able to acknowledge the possibility that some other belief may be the truth, we must then introduce a new possibility. Since Far Eastern Thought understands the power behind the universe to be an impersonal life force and not a personal, objective God, we must share the Theistic understanding of reality until the individual is able to comprehend the possibility of a personal creator God. We will have to explain who God is and what he is like. This doesn't mean the person will immediately accept it, but we cannot move to the next step until there is understanding on this point.

c. *Belief System Bridge #1: The truth about God can only be known from the Bible.*

In order to validate the Christian belief we wish to share, we need to explain the authority source of the Christian faith. If we have already led the person to an understanding of the God of the Christian faith, an explanation of the validity of the Bible is a critical next step. Now the person must understand our authority source in order to have confidence we are leading him or her in the right direction.

To do this, we will need to be conversant with the evidence for the validity of the Bible. Numerous lines of evidence support the validity of the Christian authority source. As we share our witness, we may have to go into the reasons why the Bible is the Truth.

Again, coming to an understanding of the Christian belief system does not guarantee that an FET believer is going to agree about the nature of God. It is, though, a necessary step in the process.

d. *Belief System Bridge #2: Explain the Christian Worldview*

When an individual grasps the concept that the Bible is the authority source for the Christian belief system, we must then give an overview of the Christian faith. This begins with an explanation of God's purpose in creation, then moves on to deal with the Fall, the results of the Fall, redemption, and eternity.

e. *Belief System Bridge #3: Explain the Gospel Message*

Once the person understands the big picture of the Christian faith, it then becomes possible to share the gospel message in a way that brings him or her to a decision point.

Non-Christian Theism

Theists look to some form of revelation to validate their beliefs. They believe a transcendent God has revealed himself to humanity. They then assert some scripture or prophet as the means by which the revelation is passed to mankind.

The problem we run into with Theism is that every individual theistic belief system has its own authority source and each one contradicts all others. Again, a means of arbitrating between the various belief systems is necessary.

We do have a bit of a different dynamic in Theism, though. This is the worldview system which corresponds with the way human beings actually experience reality and is our own worldview. As such, the analysis we engage with people from this background must be at the individual belief system level rather than at the worldview level. We already share a common worldview platform with them.

As Christians, we believe that the truth about God can only be known from the Bible. While ultimately this is a faith assertion, it is not purely blind faith. It is faith based on various kinds of evidence – empirical, logical and experiential.

As we delve into the various Theistic belief systems, it becomes possible to use evidence to discover the strengths of the Christian faith and the shortcomings of other beliefs. Sources for understanding God outside of the Bible are not reliable, and the evidence will bear this out.

1) Basic Assumption: There is an infinite and transcendent (supernatural) God who is the Creator and Sustainer of the material universe.

2) Major Belief Systems Within the Non-Christian Theistic Worldview:
- The Way International
- The Unity School of Christianity
- Children of God (AKA: The Family of Love)
- Jehovah's Witnesses
- The Church of Jesus Christ of Latter-day Saints (Mormons)
- Judaism
- Kabbalah
- Islam
- Baha'i
- Nation of Islam

3) Non-Christian Theism's Answers to the Essential Questions:
- What is the nature of ultimate reality? - There is a transcendent God who created and sustains the material universe for his own purposes.
- What is the nature of a human being? - Human beings are creatures which have been intentionally created by God for his own purpose.

- What is salvation and how is it achieved? - Salvation, in Theism, is defined by the particular systems. Each one has its own definition of the ultimate purpose of God and man's part in that plan. To determine salvation for Non-Christian Theists, it is necessary to study each system individually.

4) Weakness in Non-Christian Theism:

There is no generic way to expose the weaknesses of non-Christian Theistic belief systems. Each one has its own history and logical structure. We can be sure, though, that there will be historical and logical problems with each one. To get at any given system, it will be necessary to deal with that one specifically.

5) Starting Point for Witness to Non-Christian Theists:

Theists look to some form of revelation to validate their beliefs. They believe in a transcendent God who has revealed himself and his ways to humanity. They, then, latch onto some form of scripture or a prophet as the means by which that authoritative revelation is passed on to mankind. In order to effectively witness to a Theist who is not a Christian, we must lead him or her to understand the following:

a. *Worldview Bridge #1 - The truth about God can only be known from the Bible.*

Theists who are not Christians are going to have their own source of revelation that they acknowledge to be the truth. At this point, it may be necessary to research their authority source to discover its shortcomings. Sources for understanding God outside of the Bible are simply not reliable, and evidence will show that. Theists already believe in a transcendent God, so our task is simply to demonstrate that any deity other than the one revealed in the Bible is not the true God.

b. *Belief System Bridge #1 - The truth about God can only be known from the Bible and it is a reliable authority source.*

As before, we will need to explain the authority source of the Christian faith and be prepared to give evidence why it is true. There is powerful evidence that the Bible and what it says about Jesus Christ is true.

In order to make our case, we need to be conversant with the evidence for the validity of the Bible. Numerous lines of evidence support the validity of the Christian authority source. As we share our witness, we may have to go into the reasons why the Bible is the Truth.

For non-Christian Theists who claim to follow the Bible, it will be necessary to dissect their particular doctrines. We can be sure that they will use Scripture passages out of context and blatant misinterpretations to try and justify their doctrines, so our biblical interpretation skills must be sharp.

Again, coming to an understanding of the Christian belief system does not guarantee that our friend is going to agree about the nature of God, though it will be necessary for the individual to at least understand our position.

c. *Belief System Bridge #2: Explain the Christian Worldview*
When an individual grasps the concept that the Bible is the authority source for the Christian belief system, we must then give an overview of the Christian faith. This begins with an explanation of God's purpose in creation, then moves on to deal with the Fall, the results of the Fall, redemption, and eternity.

e. *Belief System Bridge #3: Explain the Gospel Message*
Once the person understands the big picture of the Christian faith, it then becomes possible to share the gospel message in a way that brings him or her to a decision point.

Hybrid Belief Systems

Some belief systems are hard to categorize because they have taken elements from two or more worldviews and attempted to combine them. The big problem is that every worldview literally contradicts every other worldview. As a result, every hybrid belief system contains irreconcilable internal contradictions. Typically, believers in hybrid systems deal with this problem by simply ignoring the contradictions.

1) Basic Assumption:
No single assumption, or set of assumptions, can be identified for hybrid belief systems. Each one has its own unique combination

of beliefs cherry-picked from two or more worldview systems. To deal with people who hold a hybrid belief, it will be necessary to study the system individually.

2) Major Hybrid Belief Systems:
- New Age
- Christian Science
- Unity School of Christianity
- Unitarian Universalism
- The Unification Church
- Scientology
- Confucianism

3) Hybrid Answers to the Essential Questions:
Hybrid belief systems have no single way to answer the three essential questions. Each one will answer them based on its particular belief set. Every one, though, will have internal contradictions that will become evident when we specifically find its answers to the three essential questions.

4) Weakness of Hybrids
Since every worldview literally contradicts every other worldview, and hybrids, by definition, take elements from more than one worldview foundation, every hybrid belief system has built in contradictory beliefs. As such, no hybrid belief system can logically hold together. By analyzing the various hybrid belief systems, we can discover which worldviews they draw from and show the contradictions which emerge. The specific contradictions relate to the particular combination represented in an individual system.

5) Starting Point for Witness to Hybrid Believers
Hybrid belief systems try to combine elements from more than one worldview into a single system. As such, every hybrid belief system has built-in contradictory beliefs. Since every worldview literally excludes every other worldview, these elements cannot help but contradict one another. In order to effectively witness to a person holding a hybrid belief system, we must lead them to understand the following:

a. *Worldview Bridge #1 - Hybrid belief systems have serious problems with their authority source.*

In order to point out the contradictions within a particular hybrid belief system, we have to study and understand the specific beliefs within that system. There are many hybrids and the specific contradictions relate to the particular combination of worldview beliefs represented in each one.

The key is to expose the weaknesses of their authority sources. As we dig into a hybrid's authority source, we will find the contradictions, as well as other problems, with the belief's validity.

b. *Worldview Bridge #2 - There exists an objective, personal God who can be known.*

Once we demonstrate that a hybrid belief is not valid, it will then be necessary to explain the Christian point of view. This will involve explaining the fact that God exists along with who he is and the truth that there is only one true God.

c. *Belief System Bridge #1 - The truth about God can only be known from the Bible.*

Once we demonstrate to the other person that his or her authority source is not valid, we have the opportunity to present our case. At this point we can present the Bible as the true revelation from God and give evidence as to why it is the truth.

If we have already led the person to understand the God of the Christian faith, an explanation of the validity of the Bible is a critical next step. Now the individual must acknowledge our authority source in order to have confidence that we are leading them in the right direction.

In order to do this, we need to be conversant with the evidence for the validity of the Bible. Numerous lines of evidence support the validity of the Christian authority source. As we share our witness, we may have to show the reasons why the Bible is the Truth.

d. *Belief System Bridge #2: Explain the Christian Worldview*

When an individual grasps the concept that the Bible is the authority source for the Christian belief system, we must then give an overview of the Christian faith. This begins with an explanation of God's purpose in creation, then moves on to deal with the Fall, the results of the Fall, redemption, and eternity.

e. Belief System Bridge #3: Explain the Gospel Message
Once the person understands the big picture of the Christian faith, it then becomes possible to share the gospel message in a way that brings him or her to a decision point.

The Importance of the Starting Point in Witness

Wendy was doing her best to share with the man at the lunch counter. However, her starting point was simply inadequate for sharing with a secular Jew.

The starting point for witness is not the gospel message itself. Before the message can be shared, we must know the worldview language of the person we wish to witness to. Just as we can't have a conversation with a person in English who doesn't speak the language, we can't share the gospel message with those who don't understand its worldview foundation – they simply will not understand what we mean.

In our modern day, more and more people simply don't understand the Christian worldview because they have their own non-Christian worldview. To share the gospel with these people, it is necessary to bridge the gap between the two. When this is effectively done, we can then share the gospel message in a way that makes sense to the hearer.

Chapter 5

The Art of Argument

"You must be crazy not to believe in God!"
"You're crazy for believing it!"
The two men sat across from one another in the office break room. Jack was trying to witness to Ron, one of his co-workers. Ron had stated strongly that he did not believe in God and did not see how anyone could. After a few minutes of bantering, the discussion devolved into an argument.
"Well, let me tell you why I think you're dumb for not believing in God," retorted Jack. He then laid out several points he had read about how atheists are ignorant of the truth and evil.
Ron just looked at him and shook his head not really knowing what else to say.
"I guess I showed you," said Jack as he headed out the door.

Rarely is anyone ever convinced to become a Christian simply by argument, especially like the one above. We certainly do have a compelling point of view that can be defended. But ultimately, a relationship with God is personal – between an individual and God. When people decide to follow Christ, we must realize that even before we ever engaged them in argument, God was already calling them to himself.
Coming to know Christ is not merely a matter of the intellectual acceptance of a set of ideas – which is what arguing compels. That

being said, we will not concede that our arguments are irrelevant. No one can legitimately accept beliefs they do not understand. God wants to use believers as a means of sharing the gospel. But when it actually comes to the point of making a decision to follow Christ, the individual does not do it by accepting an argument – he or she must accept the person of Jesus Christ.

This distinction between the personal and the impersonal is ultimately the critical point when it comes to sharing a witness. If we miss this, we may become a good debater, but we will never be a good witness.

Our purpose is not to win arguments, it is to be a faithful witness of Jesus Christ. And the goal of it all is to see other people willingly invite Christ into their lives. To see that purpose come to fruition, we must be able to make compelling arguments.

There are two approaches we can use as we make our arguments. The first takes an offensive tack. This is, perhaps, the least understood and least used method, but probably the most important when sharing with non-believers – particularly those who are antagonistic. Offensive arguing is designed to demonstrate the weaknesses of non-Christian belief systems. The second approach is defensive. This approach is the more traditional use of apologetics to give positive evidence for why we believe what we believe. This method is more useful when we wish to give evidence to those who are truly seekers, and confidence to those who are already believers.

Arguing Offensively

When talking about arguing offensively, we are not advocating that a person be offensive in their argumentation. Rather, we are speaking of not allowing oneself to be caught on the defensive. There is certainly a need to be able to defend our faith, and we should prepare ourselves in that arena. But our arguing should never be from a defensive position. We should never engage an argument without first at least putting ourselves on equal footing with our opponent.

The fact is, every belief system in existence is built on a faith foundation. That is why it is called a *belief* system. Other beliefs are just as vulnerable to problems regarding a lack of empirical proof as are we with our Christian faith. The time for a defense of our faith comes when we have the opportunity to share the positive evidence of the Christian faith. But even this must not be done from a defensive posture. We should never allow people to question the validity of our faith until they have first justified their own.

Dealing with Relationships

One of the key principles that must always be kept in mind whenever we engage another person in argument is that the one we are engaging is a person. Thus, the context of the argument is a relationship. As such, relationship is an important matter to consider.

As a Christian, the most important thing to keep in mind is that whatever you do in life is for a purpose – God's purpose. God has made it clear that his ultimate aim is to bring people into relationship with himself. If we are in tune with him, that becomes our purpose as well. So, our engagement in argument needs to be such that it is aligned with God's purpose.

This does not mean that our interactions are always congenial. Some people need to be put in their place – not just for their own sake, but also for others they intimidate or influence. Sometimes it is necessary to shock people into realizing their point of view is invalid. We have to assess each encounter to determine the appropriate approach.

So, we must keep in mind that the element of relationship is always in play. We are not trying to win arguments, we are trying to win people. Any argument that does not take this into account is not of God. For that reason, it is essential to continuously nurture our relationships to the highest degree possible. This is true no matter how an opponent responds to us.

How People Try to Put Christians on the Defensive

In order to take the offensive in our arguing, we do not have to take on a bad attitude or become overly aggressive. But we do have to put ourselves in a good position to argue.

When non-believers attack Christians for their beliefs, they commonly do several things. Virtually every attack begins with the assumption that something is wrong with the Christian faith in relation to their own beliefs. These snipers assume that they have a morally or intellectually superior position and, based on that assumption, they go on the attack.

Unfortunately, most Christians simply allow this attack to happen. But the truth is, there is no reason to allow it. We can preemptively put the other person on the defensive if we clearly understand their belief.

One common way non-Christians put Christians on the defensive is to call us hypocrites. How many times have you heard someone say they would never go to church because it is full of hypocrites? Well, this may be true. But a couple of other things are true, as well. First, the presence of hypocrites does not determine the truth or falsity of the Christian faith. Our faith can be true even if everyone in a particular church is a hypocrite. In addition, hypocrites are everywhere – including the circles where the accuser happens to roam. How silly would it be to never see a doctor again because some doctors are hypocrites? How crazy to never go fishing, hunting, or walking, to never watch sports or go to work again because some who do those activities are hypocrites? And how ridiculous is it to allow the bad actions or attitudes of others to determine our own faith? Frankly, people using this attack are simply making excuses.

A second common means some non-believers use to put Christians on the defensive is to say that science proves the Bible is not true. Usually, this kind of attack focuses on the Theory of Evolution and comes from those who believe it, though not exclusively.

To be blunt, this assertion is simply false. Science does not prove the Bible is not true any more than it proves the Bible is true. And while science can validate or invalidate certain specific facts that a particular belief system may claim, it is incapable of proving that any set of beliefs is false. Specifically, as regards The Theory of Evolution, science does not give positive proof for that particular faith position either. In fact, a lot of scientific data actually challenges the validity of the theory.

A third technique some non-believers use to put Christians on the defensive is to assert that the Bible is not reliable – that it contains a lot of errors. This is another red herring. Numerous passages in the Bible certainly are difficult to interpret, but people who denigrate the Bible this way are actually showing their own ignorance regarding the principles of biblical interpretation, or their laziness by not doing the work of an interpreter.

A fourth way non-believers try to get the upper hand is to strongly assert their own beliefs. Usually this is done without anything to actually back it up. They just smoothly talk "as if" what they are saying is true. They often get away with it because they are more fully versed in their beliefs than the Christian is in his or hers. This confidence factor alone tends to silence the Christian who doesn't know how to answer back.

All four of these issues can be dealt with by Christians in short order – if they have done their due diligence. A little study to get up to speed on the topics mentioned will stop this kind of put-down. The big problem is not that these issues can't be addressed, but that most Christians simply don't put forth enough effort to understand them.

Problems in Non-Christian Belief Systems

The fact is, every non-Christian belief system has its own severe credibility problems. We must be able to identify those problems and point them out when others try to put us on the defensive. This approach does not prove our position over that of others. What it does, though, is put us on equal footing with them. At that point, we can deal with the evidence related to the veracity of the belief rather than with put-downs. Let's look briefly at the major problems related to the various non-Christian worldviews.

1. Naturalism

We must remember that there are many Naturalistic belief systems. Some have their own unique weaknesses that can be added to what is mentioned here. That being said, every one of them has the same underlying foundation, and the weaknesses of that foundation are inherent in each one.

In analyzing Naturalistic belief systems, we first see that all of them look to human reason as their authority source. Since they acknowledge no transcendent reality, they are forced to assert that unaided human reason can lead to a definitive understanding of objective reality. The only problem is that unaided reason cannot prove any belief system. If you look at the foundation of any faith system, it rests entirely on how it answers the seven worldview questions (see Appendix 3). As it turns out, the answer to every worldview question is based on faith. There is no empirical answer for any one of them. Since the Naturalist asserts that ultimately everything can be explained empirically, they immediately face a logical dilemma.

At its most basic level, Naturalism must assert that:
- matter has a natural source,
- life can emerge out of non-life,
- less developed life forms can evolve into more complex forms, and
- consciousness can emerge out of non-consciousness.

The dilemma is that no science supports any of these assertions. All of them are faith assumptions. It simply cannot be demonstrated that the supernatural does not exist or that natural processes alone account for what does exist. So, Naturalism asserts that it is possible to get at reality using empirical methodology, but its understanding of the nature of reality must be believed based on blind faith.

2. Animism

As with Naturalism, there are many Animistic belief systems. And as was true with Naturalism, individual Animistic belief systems have their own unique weaknesses. But the same principle applies here as before – all have the same underlying foundation, so the weaknesses found in the foundation are inherent in them all.

As we look at Animism's authority foundation, we find that this worldview is built completely on history and tradition. Animists believe that the nature of reality is expressed in the beliefs which have been passed down by the ancestors from generation to generation. There is no other basis, and this foundation is not questioned in any respect. Animists see the outworking of the gods in nature and don't perceive a need to look to any other source – such as revelation or science.

As such, the Animistic position has nothing to support it. We see many different historical situations in the various Animistic traditions around the world. Any particular belief system is only one among many which literally contradict one another on key points. This leads to the obvious conclusion that they cannot all be true.

That being the case, there must be some way of arbitrating between the different systems. The problem is that there is no way to make this determination. All any system has is anecdotal evidence to back it up – and the interpretation of the evidence depends completely on its presuppositions.

So the question must be raised: How can any group know their belief structure is true and opposing beliefs are false? Something is not true simply because someone believes it. History and tradition are simply not sufficient to prove the truth of a belief system.

3. Far Eastern Thought

The same issues seen in both Naturalism and Animism also hold true with the numerous Far Eastern Thought belief systems. Every one of them has its own unique weaknesses. And still true here is the fact that the weaknesses found in the underlying foundation apply to them all.

Far Eastern Thought belief systems rely primarily on human experience as their authority source to validate their worldview assumptions. They take beliefs passed down through the ages and filter them through personal experience.

When we examine the problems of Far Eastern Thought, we find the same foundational issue that existed for Animism, only with a different authority source. In Animism, the problem related to contradictory traditions with no way to arbitrate between them. The same problem is true of human experience. People from various Far Eastern Thought belief systems experience reality in contradictory ways. So, who arbitrates between the contradictory experiences of the different belief systems? Once again, something is not true simply because someone has a certain kind of experience. Truth is an objective reality which can be affirmed in some ways by experience, but not proven by it. Human experience is simply not sufficient to assert the truth of a belief system.

4. Non-Christian Theism

As with all of the worldview platforms cited before, there are many Theistic belief systems. And, as before, each one has its own problematic issues – but in this case with a slight difference. Theism is the worldview foundation most closely aligned with the way human beings actually experience reality. It acknowledges both physical and spiritual dimensions of reality and is able to reconcile the two together.

The problem, though, is that every Theistic belief system claims its own God is the true one. But all of them can't be right. In fact, only one can possibly be right. God exists in a particular way as a particular person, and any belief asserting something different is necessarily wrong.

The authority source for every Theistic belief system is some form of revelation. A transcendent God is acknowledged to exist and is believed to have revealed himself to mankind – generally by some scripture or prophet.

So to find the truth, it is necessary to analyze each individual belief system's authority source based on the logic of its own worldview foundation. In doing this, the belief system's problems will become evident based on inaccuracies in the historical record, inconsistent logic, contradictions within the authority source, and the like. As Christians, we affirm that these kinds of problems are evident in every non-Christian Theistic belief system.

5. Hybrid Belief Systems

The definition of a hybrid belief system is any belief that tries to combine elements from two or more worldviews into a single system. The problem, as we have repeatedly shown, is that every worldview literally contradicts every other worldview. As such, all hybrid belief systems have automatic internal contradictions. For instance, it is not possible for God to exist and not exist at the same time. God cannot be personal and impersonal at the same time. Every hybrid system has some kind of internal contradiction of this magnitude.

In dealing with people who hold hybrid belief systems, all that is necessary is to figure out where the contradictions lie. Once that is done, the belief system is effectively eliminated as a legitimate way of understanding the truth about the structure of reality.

Do Your Due Diligence

The ability to operate on the offensive, rather than from a defensive posture, requires doing our due diligence. We must become knowledgeable enough to counter the attacks of whoever comes up against us. So, just what is this body of knowledge? There are four important matters.

First we must master an understanding of worldview. Every person we ever want to share the gospel with already has some worldview belief. It may be relatively close to the truth, or it may be way off base. Whatever it is, we need to understand it because it will affect the way we share the gospel message. Without an understanding of worldview, it is difficult to know the correct starting point for witness.

Secondly, we need to understand the content of the gospel message itself. This means that we must be able to tell people:
- who God is,
- the nature of humanity as separated from God because of sin,
- how God provided a fix for the sin problem, and
- what we can do to make that fix a personal reality for our own lives.

The message is not difficult or complicated, but we must take the time and effort to learn the material. We will not be in a position to ever bring anyone to a knowledge of faith in Christ without this knowledge.

Thirdly, we must master relationships. Certainly, some people are naturally better at making new relationships than others. But that is not the point. We all have relationships, or potential relationships, with people we interact with every day. If we wish to share our faith, we have to develop relationships which allow us to discuss religion. Even someone not very good at making relationships can learn the skills necessary to do this.

Finally, we must grasp the techniques which allow us to operate on the offensive. These techniques must include the following matters.

1. We must be able to deconstruct opposing belief systems.

Deconstructing our opponent's beliefs must be done before constructing our own for them. If they don't see a problem with their own beliefs, they will have no reason to listen to an explanation of another one. Every non-Christian belief system represents a faith position that does not reflect the truth about the nature of reality. And every one can be deconstructed to show why. When opponents make incorrect statements, we can point these out and reply with a correct one.

2. We must never allow people to evaluate the Christian faith based on assumptions from other worldviews.

A person who evaluates Christianity based on Naturalistic assumptions, for example, will dismiss out of hand every miracle mentioned in the Bible. This would include certain core beliefs such as the virgin birth and the resurrection of Christ, or even that a supernatural God exists. A person cannot become a Christian without believing in the faith's core beliefs. If someone insists on making attacks of this nature, it will probably be necessary to deconstruct their worldview platform before we can even have a respectable dialogue.

3. We must learn how to hold people accountable for their attacks on our faith.

When someone attacks us, it is important to make them back up the attack. The attacks can come from numerous directions but, regardless of any particular point they make, we must make them explain why it is valid. Some of the points they try to make may include denigrating the validity of the Bible, putting down Christians as hypocrites or ignoramuses, accusing Christianity of being anti-science, and the like. It is important to recognize, though, that every attack can be intelligently answered. We must make our attackers defend the validity of their assaults before we dignify them with an answer.

4. We must always argue to the end, to the highest degree possible.

Sometimes a discussion can become tedious or uncomfortable for any of a number of reasons. If that happens, we should not fall prey to the temptation to simply cut out of the discussion. If we do, it is quite possible that our discussion partner will think they have won. We need to stick with them until they finally give up. This attitude of sticking it out to the end is not for the purpose of simply winning an argument. Rather, it is to make sure that our opponent recognizes that he or she cannot avoid the ultimate truth. If we have done our due diligence, we cannot be out maneuvered because the Christian faith really does represent the truth about the nature of reality. The truth always rises to the top when given the opportunity. If issues come up that we personally don't know how to deal with, we must seek out the answers. Don't give up!

5. We must never make personal attacks on our opponents.

It is important to not miss opportunities to point out the flaws and inconsistencies of attacks against our argument, even strongly if necessary. But it must never become personal – that is, we must not call our opponent ugly names or impugn their character. Even if they begin throwing insults, we should never insult back. Simply point out that their personal insults do not contribute to making their point. Our ultimate goal is not to beat people down, but to share a witness of Jesus Christ. How the witness is received is ultimately up to the person we are interacting with, not ourselves. But if offense is taken, it should not be because we have made a personal attack. It may be that we have pinned them into a corner and they are mad that they can't answer back. Even though they may accuse us of a personal attack, or lash out in a personal attack on us, it is okay. We can gently point out that we have not personally attacked them and that they should not do it to us either.

It is difficult to keep from being on the defensive without making the effort to become skilled in arguing offensively. But, with a mastery of offensive arguing, dealing with hostile people can be a productive opportunity to build the kingdom of God.

Arguing Defensively
Being on the defensive is never a good idea. But there are those times when we must step up and defend the tenets of the Christian faith. In fact, an entire field of study, called apologetics, is dedicated to doing just that. This kind of defense is a very important skill for Christians. But, as important as it is, its value only comes into play once we have established that our faith is worthy of defense by demonstrating the faith nature of our opponent's position. In other words, there is a huge distinction between arguing from a defensive posture and defending our faith. We should always be ready to defend it, but we should never allow ourselves to be on the defensive.

It is always good to keep in mind that even this is a part of the witnessing process. Defending the faith is not simply a matter of sharing intellectual material. Its purpose is always to lead people to Jesus Christ. This is most valuable when sharing with people who are open to the evidence for the Christian faith.

So, once we establish that our faith is worthy of defense, how should we go about doing it? Essentially, it is a matter of sharing the evidence for the validity of our faith. We should become familiar with all of the basic lines of evidence. None is, by itself, proof that our faith is the truth about the nature of reality. After all, we are working with worldview beliefs. But piled layer upon layer, these lines of evidence can be quite compelling.

We will take a moment here to look over the various categories of evidence. We need to keep in mind that this is only a brief summary. Entire books could be, and have been, written about each of these. But we at least need to know the categories.

Evidence for the Validity of the Bible

Many people attack the Christian faith by attacking the Bible. These attacks fall into several categories.

1. Preservation and Transmission of the Text

Some critics say the Bible is an ancient book and was not accurately preserved and transmitted over the centuries. But, the fact is, the Bible has been accurately preserved and transmitted to us throughout the ages. An entire discipline of study is dedicated to tracking the Bible's transmission, and the evidence for its accuracy is overwhelming. Anyone making the argument that the Bible has not been transmitted accurately to our time simply does not know what they are talking about.

2. Contradictions

Another attack people make is that the Bible is full of contradictions. Skeptics who make this attack are again in error. In order to make this claim, they must filter the Bible's teachings through their own worldview beliefs. This is not an acceptable methodology. The consistency of the Bible must be based on its own teachings and its own worldview foundation. Even though it was written by approximately 40 authors over about a 1500 year period in different languages, places and cultures, the Bible is entirely consistent with itself.

3. Unfulfilled Prophesy

A third attack is the claim that prophesies contained in the Bible have not been fulfilled. This argument takes a number of different forms, so it is necessary to be knowledgeable in this area to make an adequate defense. It is also important to note that various groups of Christians make differing claims about prophesy based on diverse approaches to the study of theology and eschatology. It is critical to sort these things out before engaging an argument in this arena. That being said, the Bible contains literally scores of prophesies that have been fulfilled in minute detail. Some of them were made hundreds of years before the fulfillment.

4. Science Disproves the Bible

Finally, some people claim that science disproves the Bible. In actual fact, science supports the Bible in virtually every way.

One area of science that gives positive evidence for the validity of the Bible is archaeology. Over the years, it has provided increasing evidence that the places mentioned in the Bible actually existed and the events recorded in the Bible are historically accurate.

Other areas where science upholds the Bible relate to the existence of an intelligent designer and the creation of life by God (as opposed to Naturalistic evolution).

Identity Evidence

The Christian faith stands or falls on the truth that Christ was who he said he was – the Messiah of God – God in the flesh. If he was who he claimed to be, the truth of the Christian faith is assured. In fact, Jesus completely conforms to the identity of Messiah from prophesy. Beyond that, his life stands the test. He actually lived up to what he taught.

In dealing with this issue, it is important to note that Jesus Christ believed that he, himself, was God. He was either crazy, lying or truthful. The evidence is compelling that he was telling the truth. (Matt. 20:225-28, Mark 2:6-12, Luke 22:67-71, John 4:25-26, Rev. 1:17-18, and many more.)

Beyond that, eyewitnesses who lived and worked with Jesus also believed he was God. They believed this not merely on the basis of Jesus telling it to them, but on the basis of his whole body of work in their presence – both his teachings and miracles. (Matt. 28:9, John 1:1, Acts 7:55-60, Romans 10:13-14, 1:Cor. 1:1-2, Phil. 2:5-11, Col. 2:9, Heb. 1:6, and many more.)

Eyewitness Evidence

One of the strongest lines of evidence for the validity of the Christian faith is eyewitness accounts. The people who knew Jesus and were present as he taught and performed miracles were the same ones who wrote the gospels and other New Testament writings. Not only do we have these eyewitness accounts, we have biographies of the life and teachings of Christ. And, as we stated before, these writings were accurately preserved and transmitted over the course of the centuries.

Corroborating Evidence
While corroborating evidence is not hugely extensive, references to Jesus are found in various historical writings outside of the biblical text. While these references are not reliable in the sense of giving testimony of Jesus' messiahship, they are significant in that historically Jesus made a big enough impact on the world of his day to warrant being included in those histories. He was an actual person in history who caused enough of a stir to be mentioned.

Rebuttal Evidence
Over the years, some of the greatest non-believing minds have tried many approaches to discredit the Christian faith. Some have tried to deny Jesus' historical existence, negate his resurrection, discredit his teachings, repudiate his miracles, prove God does not exist, or used other means. But the fact is, not a single approach used to discount the evidence for the truth of the Gospel can stand up to scrutiny.

Medical Evidence
As it turns out, the writer of one of the biographies of Jesus was a doctor. Granted, we don't have a description of Jesus' death based on modern medicine (since modern medical technology did not exist in those days). Nonetheless, the descriptions of the death and resurrection of Jesus are consistent with what would be expected based on the medical knowledge of that day.

Evidence of the Missing Body
Many nay-sayers have formulated all kinds of theories to explain what happened to the body of Jesus after his resurrection. Virtually every attempt to discredit Jesus' resurrection from the dead begins with the Naturalistic assumption that, since the supernatural does not exist, his body could not have been resurrected. Their reasoning is that since a resurrection was impossible there had to be another

explanation for the empty tomb. But these skeptics cannot provide any definitive proof of their point. The fact is, after the resurrection of Christ, the body really was gone out of the grave.

The Evidence of Jesus' Post-resurrection Appearances

If the missing body was the only issue, detractors could claim that followers of Jesus simply hid the body well enough that others never found it. However, there is more. After his resurrection, Jesus appeared to his followers live and in person for a period of forty days. Again, it was the people who actually witnessed these appearances who were the authors of most of the New Testament writings. During that time, Jesus was seen by the apostles, close associates and others – in all, over 500 people.

Circumstantial Evidence

Several lines of evidence fall into the category of being circumstantial. Each taken by itself may not amount to much, but together they are another powerful indicator of the validity of the Christian faith.

First, we have the fact that after the ascension, the disciples were willing to die for their beliefs. No one will put their life on the line for a lie. Had the whole thing about Jesus been a lie, when it came down to either living or dying because of the beliefs, most people would have either recanted or simply faded into the background. However, tradition has it that all of the disciples but one died a martyr's death.

A second line of evidence relates to the conversion of skeptics. In particular, two very high profile skeptics not only became believers after meeting Jesus following his resurrection, but became leaders in the new movement.

One was James, the brother of Jesus. We can only imagine how difficult it must have been to finally come to the conclusion that your own brother could be the Messiah of God who had been prophesied in Scripture.

The second skeptic who turned believer was Saul of Tarsus. Originally, he was violently opposed to the faith – even to the point of being a leading persecutor of Christians. However, after a personal encounter with the risen Christ, Saul (AKA: Paul) believed and became a follower. Later he wrote a large portion of what is now the New Testament.

Another line of circumstantial evidence focuses on the changes which occurred in key social structures, and the introduction of a completely new theology among former Jews. The kinds of things Jewish believers gave up were so central to their identity as Jews that it is inconceivable that they would do it without some kind of radical evidence. And literally thousands experienced the evidence.

A fourth line of circumstantial evidence concerns the ordinances of The Lord's Supper and baptism. We would not expect that the celebration of an execution and a curse would become the focal point of a belief system. Yet this is precisely what happened.

Finally, the emergence of the church from a small band of Christ followers to a worldwide movement is nothing less than astounding. It is virtually unheard of for a belief system to emerge and grow as this one did without any kind of violent coercion.

Experiential Evidence

This last line of evidence is very personal. That being said, it is ultimately the one which must be accepted above all others. No kind of empirical proof is capable of changing a person's life. Those kinds of proofs cause a person think about other possibilities, but conversion to the Christian faith is a personal event which has to be experienced on a personal level. God is a person, and becoming a Christian requires that an individual enter into a personal relationship with him through faith. No amount of intellectual knowledge, or any other impersonal means, will get the job done.

In addressing this level of evidence, the first thing we should point to is the fact that our own lives (the authors of this book) have been changed by knowing Jesus Christ in a personal relationship. We have met him and interact with him personally on a continual basis.

Also, we can point to the millions and millions of others throughout history whose lives have been changed because of their personal relationship with God through Jesus Christ. Again, this line of evidence does not stand on its own, but, added to all of the other evidence, it is a very powerful piece of the puzzle.

The Value of Argument

When we use the word "argument" in the current context, we are not talking about being contentious. Rather, we are speaking of sharing a witness. The arguments are designed to shake people out of rebellion against God and to share with them why Christ is the door to knowing him. If we keep our purpose in mind and approach this with the right attitude, God will use our lives to lead others into a saving relationship with himself.

Part III - The Practice of Christian Witness

Chapter 6 - Sharing an Effective Witness Presentation
Chapter 7 - Witnessing in Daily Life

Chapter 6

Sharing an Effective Witness Presentation

John, a Christian, had been meeting weekly with his friend Albert for several months. They had met at a business conference and discovered a common interest in motorcycles. In the course of their conversations and riding trips, John learned that Albert had been raised Jewish but was not observant. John had concluded that Albert was, in fact, a Naturalist who didn't really believe in anything supernatural. They had talked at length about the difference between a naturalistic worldview and a theistic one, and John felt he had made progress in exposing to Albert the logical flaws in his thinking. Albert even acknowledged that maybe a god existed after all, but he didn't see how it was relevant to his life.

John felt that he was finally at a point where he could share the gospel of Christ with Albert. So he gently led their discussions to the issue of who Jesus was and why it mattered for his eternal destiny. Albert listened to what his friend said and weighed his words carefully.

Like John, perhaps we are now at the place where we actually get to share the gospel message. We are assuming, here, that we have established the necessary relationship with a person who is ready to hear us explain the message of how to be saved.

At this point, it is important to recognize that the amount of information we share and the way we present it may vary according to the person we are witnessing to. Those who already essentially understand the message will not need nearly as much explanation as those who are further away, in order to bring them to the point of decision. But by knowing the full scope of the possibilities, it is possible to share an effective witness no matter what the situation. Let's take a moment to look at the parts of the process for sharing a gospel presentation.

1. Get People into the Presentation

Every person we ever witness to has a belief system already in place. When we share a witness, the first order of business is to establish a relationship with the person which can provide a means of bridging the gap from what he or she believes to the truth of the gospel message. This was the entire point of chapter four as we dealt with the starting point of witness.

Some of the people we interact with will already be close to understanding the gospel message. They may be people who grew up in church or at least had a family which claimed to be Christian. On the other end of the spectrum are those who know nothing about Jesus and grew up immersed in a different worldview environment. And, of course, all shades of belief are in between. The first step in witness is to be in a position to engage the other person long enough to share an effective gospel presentation.

In some cases we can do this in a "one shot deal." We "cold call" in some form, share the gospel, and get out. Even with a cold call witness, though, the person has to be engaged and agree to listen to the presentation. That kind of relationship is shallow and temporary, but must still be established. More often than not, though, it will take time to cultivate a relationship to the point where the person trusts us enough to open up about faith issues.

So, regardless of the situation, the first step is to establish a relationship which leads to an opening to share the gospel. This may happen quickly or may take years. It may be done based on sales skills that have been acquired by training and experience or in the natural flow of life and making friends. Or it may just emerge from being a friend to someone over the course of time. But until this relationship is established, it is impossible to move on to the next step.

2. Distinguish Non-Christian Belief from Christian Belief

The key to bridging the gap between the beliefs of the one we wish to witness to and the Christian faith is to make a comparison between the two. When we have that comparison in place, it becomes possible to do an analysis to determine how each one lines up with empirical knowledge, logic, and human experience. To do this, all that is necessary is to answer the essential questions for both of the belief systems (Who is God? What is a human being? What comprises salvation and how does one achieve it?) and lay them side by side for comparison.

The most dramatic differences, obviously, will be between belief systems which come from different worldviews. But even when there are common beliefs, a perceptible difference exists between the Christian faith and any non-Christian belief system.

The reason for this is that the Christian faith is the objective truth about reality and every other belief system strays from that objective truth. Some beliefs stray far away and the difference is easily seen. Others may be close but still be over the line and out of true Christianity.

Regardless of the distance between our Christian faith and that of the person we wish to witness to, making the distinction is absolutely critical. It is this difference that demonstrates who needs to be witnessed to and determines the starting point for sharing the witness.

3. Explain the Scope of the Christian Worldview

It is possible to accept Christ without understanding everything about the Christian worldview. But it is nearly impossible to maintain total confidence in the faith without it. The Christian faith exists as a complete narrative, and without knowing the entire story some things about it don't make much sense. Many people these days are antagonistic toward our faith. Without understanding the whole story it is very difficult to answer their taunts in an intelligent way. On the other hand, if we know the whole story, we are in a position to answer any question they throw out.

The story of the Bible can be broken down into five parts: Creation, the Fall, Life after the Fall, Redemption and Eternity. If we share this story as a part of our witnessing process, our witness becomes understandable, even to people with worldviews far from our own. Let's look briefly at the Christian story.

Creation

In order to truly grasp the significance of the Christian faith, it is necessary to begin before the creation of the material universe and delve into the very mind of God. Nothing else about the Christian faith ultimately makes sense without understanding the purpose of God in the creation.

We can comprehend God's purpose because he has revealed it in Scripture (the Bible). Without this revelation it would be impossible to know anything about God. In particular, God's revelation in Scripture is essential to define his purpose in creating mankind in the first place.

The beginning of the Christian story has its roots in the creation of mankind. Before God created man in his own image, there were no created beings which fit into this category. There were other created beings, but they did not have the characteristic of being created in the image of God.

In order to grasp the significance of the creation, we must first understand something about God himself. God, as he has existed in eternity, is a real person with a real purpose in his own heart and mind. He is a unique person who contains within himself elements of both unity and diversity. This kind of "beingness" does not exist outside of the infinite and eternal person of God. He is a unity in that he is the one and only God. At the same time, he exists in diversity in that he is a Trinitarian person able to have an actual, viable relationship within his tri-personhood.

At some point, though, God made the decision to create another class of being which would have the personhood characteristics of God himself. This does not mean that he set out to create another god. Rather, he created a creature with personhood characteristics which provided the possibility of a relationship with him. God did not reveal why he made that decision. Perhaps he simply wanted another way to express his love – which is an essential part of his being. Not that this was necessary for him. As a Trinitarian being, everything he needed, including the need for relationship, is contained within himself. All we know is that he made the decision to create this new creature and he did it. With the creation of this new creature, a unique being came into existence capable of sharing a personal relationship with him.

So, at this point, we can see God's purpose in the creation of mankind. However, for that purpose to become a reality, a place for this being to live had to be made. So God created the material universe where this new creature would live. Before this creative event, there was no such thing as the material reality that we now know. God conceived of it in his own mind and created it out of nothing.

Within that material universe, God made one place perfectly capable of sustaining the physical life of this new creature. Earth was that place. And when it was ready for man, it was a literal paradise. It was God's purpose that he and man would physically enjoy one another's company eternally in this place. To achieve his purpose, God manifested himself as a physical being on this physical earth in order to share fellowship with his new creature. Of course, he was still God in eternity and was not limited to his earthly manifestation, but he did accommodate himself to the earth to fulfill his purpose.

So out of his purpose, and when the earth was ready, God created mankind in his own image. The idea of being created in the image of God simply means that man would have the personhood attributes of God. This included such things as the ability to be self-aware, creative, capable of knowledge, having a free will, and the like.

The first being that God created in this process was Adam, the first man. Adam was soon followed by the first woman, Eve. With this creation, God was able to, and did, have fellowship with a creature like himself.

In the beginning, mankind was perfect. There was no sin and no sin nature to pollute the new creation God had established. In those days, God and man physically interacted with one another on the physical earth without interference. They enjoyed intimate and unrestricted fellowship in the paradise that was Earth.

The Fall

The concept of the Fall gets to the very heart of the human condition. It helps us understand why human beings are separated from God, and why it is so difficult for us to live a life in close personal fellowship with him. It also gives us an understanding of our very nature. Knowing these things is essential for understanding ourselves and what is necessary to repair our separation from God.

Before going more deeply into this matter, an important point must be emphasized. The Fall, and the events following the Fall which God put in place to create a fix, are not mere spiritual concepts. All of this happened in actual history. The Fall and redemption from sin are actual matters that humanity must deal with in the physical existence in which we live. We are not just dealing with internal struggles as we try to think and live rightly in daily life. An actual element is in play which must be dealt with and overcome. Our internal tendency to sin leads to actual expressions of sin in life. This internal tendency is our sin nature inherited from Adam. The sin nature causes us to commit actual sins. It is what theologians call "original sin." These acts can be mental (greed, lust, anger, etc.) or physical (stealing, sexual immorality, murder, etc.). The main point, though, is that all of these things are actual elements which play out in literal history and which place genuine guilt on our lives which must be resolved.

In the beginning, as was dealt with in the previous section, God created a being capable of interacting with him in a personal relationship, and who would willfully return his love. The relationship that God had with the first man and woman in the initial stages exactly fit God's purpose. It was completely intimate and unhindered. God and man enjoyed perfect fellowship as they lived together in the earthly paradise that he had created.

Unfortunately, there came a time when Adam and Eve willfully disobeyed God and did the one thing that could break fellowship with him. When God placed them in the garden, he gave specific instructions that they could eat of any fruit they found except one. Everything was fine until one day when they made the decision to disobey this one restriction.

The thought to disobey was not their own, however. Another player entered the scene and set up the betrayal. This fact does not take away from the guilt of Adam and Eve for their disobedience. They could have made the choice to obey God, but didn't.

On that fateful day, Satan, the leader of a band of angels who had rebelled against God and was kicked out of heaven, took the form of a beautiful serpent and approached Eve with the idea of eating the forbidden fruit. His portrayal of that act convinced her that doing so was not a bad thing at all. In fact, his deception was that this fruit was exceedingly good to the point that it would make them like God himself. As it turned out, this temptation was strong enough to entice Eve, then Adam, to do the one thing God told them not to do.

The result of that act, in one way, was what Satan said it would be. It gave Adam and Eve an experiential knowledge of moral good and evil. However, Satan did not tell them the whole story. This introduction of evil created a situation where paradise itself was corrupted and caused the destruction of the unrestricted fellowship that Adam and Eve had enjoyed with God. God refuses to fellowship with sin.

It would have been bad enough if this separation from God had only affected the lives of Adam and Eve. But the results were even more widespread. The evil that entered the created order penetrated to the very core of humanity in general. As a result, the nature of mankind was infected with sin. Every human being born since that time has inherited that sin nature. This nature predisposes us to express sin through our lives in the way we think and act. As a result, all human beings are separated from God because of this evil within. God simply will not allow himself to fellowship with unholiness.

But the results of this Fall had an even wider result than the separation of man from intimate fellowship with God. As it turned out, evil was not just a spiritual concept. It had a physical manifestation which also affected the material universe God originally created as a perfect paradise. The result was the instability of the natural universe in such things as earthquakes, volcanoes tornados, hurricanes, floods, wildfires, and the like.

At this point, it might be helpful to give a more graphic characterization of sin. In some ways it is like some kind of spiritual radiation. Much like physical radiation, it literally penetrates the entirety of the created order – only it is a spiritual element, not physical. Since the Fall, this "spiritual radiation" has permeated and corrupted everything in the physical universe. In our human existence, we are conceived in an environment where we are personally affected. As such, it plays out in every element of our existence – most prominently in our tendency to live in rebellion against God.

The Fall had a spiritual root but it resulted in catastrophic physical manifestations, as well. The evil that it brought into God's created order caused mankind to take on a sin nature which separated him from intimate fellowship with God and caused the natural universe to begin to come apart.

Life after the Fall

We have already introduced the existence of the Fall and the problems it created. But to appreciate the full significance of this event, we need to address the results of this terrible tragedy in more detail.

After sin entered the world, it became the primary principle which ruled the universe. The ultimate result was that it corrupted the perfect creation God had made.

First, it created a separation between man and God. One primary characteristic of God is that he is holy – without moral blemish. The nature of holiness is such that he will not dwell in the presence of sin – that which is unholy. So, when the first humans opened the door and allowed sin to enter their being, God would no longer remain present with them. They not only committed a sinful act (an act of rebellion against God), they created a situation where sin became part of the fabric of their being. God would not dwell with them under these circumstances.

But sin not only became a part of the fabric of human existence, it also penetrated the entire created order. The universe, which was in perfect harmony from the time of its creation, was jolted out of kilter. The physical result of this entry of sin was to make the earth, indeed the entire physical universe, subject to decay and degradation.

From the very beginning, however, God was determined to repair it. He could have chosen simply to destroy it and start over. But God was not about to allow himself to be defeated by Satan and his followers – those who had already rebelled against him and who were instrumental in initiating the Fall. So, he devised a plan to redeem his fallen creation.

The fix, though, would not happen at the snap of a finger. The Fall had resulted from an act in history, so God designed the fix also to work through a historical process. This process would accomplish the purpose for which he had originally made the creation.

God intended, from the beginning, that the first man and woman would fully populate his creation. The Fall did not prevent that from happening, but it did skew the process.

The first problem introduced was physical death. With physical death, the possibility emerged that some of the beings who were created in his image would not ultimately enjoy eternity in God's created paradise. If they entered eternity in a state of separation from him because of sin, there would be no recourse to restore that relationship.

The second problem was spiritual death – eternal separation from God. Since God created mankind as a free-will creature with the ability to choose whether or not to enter a relationship with himself, some people could choose not to follow him. So, at physical death, the ultimate destination of individual human beings is settled based on the choices they make during physical life. Those who choose God in physical life will enjoy eternity with him, while those who choose not to follow him will be eternally separated from him.

Throughout history, mankind has struggled with the consequences of the Fall. We struggle with the effects of sin in the physical world such as earthquakes, tornados, hurricanes and other natural disasters. We also deal with sin's effects in human life. It wreaks havoc in society in such ways as poverty, war, abortion, homosexuality and many other problems. And finally, we face sin's effects individually as we struggle to know God and interact with him in an environment which makes that difficult.

Satan has a powerful influence in the fallen world. He is a personal presence in the world and the father of sin. He not only got the sin ball rolling, he keeps it going using every trick he can to entice individuals to follow him and rebel against God. Mankind will struggle with sin until the time is fulfilled for God to end the time of fallenness.

Redemption

We have already touched on the concept of redemption – God's restoration of his fallen creation – but we need to more fully understand how God's fix applies to our lives personally. When God saw that Satan had invaded his creation and injected the sin virus in an attempt to destroy it, God could have destroyed the world and started over. However, he chose a different path. Rather than allow that the Evil One had defeated him, God decided to overcome Satan and, in the process, fix (redeem) his creation. He provided mankind a means of salvation, and will ultimately create a new heaven and new earth from the carcass of the old.

To do this, God began a process to reverse the effects of sin introduced at the Fall. This process began with God's decision to send a redeemer into the world who would offer himself as a sacrifice in place of those separated from God because of their sin. This redeemer would have to be completely without sin and, thus, worthy of this position. As no other being was qualified, God determined that he, himself, would be this redeemer.

As the infection of sin had permeated the entire created order, the fix would also require removal of sin from the material universe, and at the same time accomplish the original purpose of the creation. Since the original purpose was to populate a perfect earth with creatures to fellowship with him, God allowed the process of procreation to proceed. Only those individuals, however, who choose to spend eternity with him are allowed the privilege of this fellowship. Those not choosing this path are destined to spend eternity outside of his presence.

As the history of the earth moved forward, God continuously revealed to mankind how to have this relationship with him. He revealed himself in nature, in the consciences of individual human beings, through specially called persons whom he divinely inspired to write Scripture, through the incarnation of Jesus Christ, and by his Holy Spirit, directly indwelling individuals who acknowledge him. This process of revelation, though, was progressive in nature.

The initial revelation was given directly to Adam and Eve and in the moral consciences of all their descendants. Through the outworking of history, God revealed the nature of the redemptive process. He chose the nation of Israel as keepers of the message and gave them the sacrificial system to be practiced in the temple. This system did not literally provide for the forgiveness of sin, as the animals being sacrificed were not capable of actually taking sin onto themselves. It did, however, foreshadow the actual sacrifice that would occur in the fullness of God's timing.

The actual sacrifice occurred when Jesus Christ was crucified on the cross. Jesus was not an ordinary man, but was God who stepped out of heaven and put on skin. Before manifesting himself as a human being, Jesus was the Son – the second person of the Trinity. When he came to earth, he was born in the normal way human beings are born. His conception was unique, however. He was not the product of the intimacy of a human man and woman. God performed a miracle, impregnating the Virgin Mary by the Holy Spirit in order that Jesus could be conceived in her womb. This was necessary so he could be born without the sin nature which is part and parcel of natural human existence.

In order for a person to qualify as the sacrifice for the sin of mankind, it was necessary for that individual to be sinless from birth to death. Thus, Jesus lived a sinless life which qualified him to become the sacrifice for the sins of mankind.

When he was finally crucified, he fulfilled God's requirements for undoing the sin problem. This process was not merely for saving mankind, it was for completely reversing all the effects of the Fall. In his redemptive work, Christ provided redemption for the entire sin infected created order – mankind as well as the physical universe. God demonstrated his power to accomplish this task with Christ's resurrection. Thus, the completion of the redemptive process was sealed.

At the time of the resurrection, however, the entire redemptive process was not yet fulfilled. The full number of human beings God desired to populate his creation was not yet complete. As a result, everything is currently in place for the culmination of God's plan. We are now only waiting for the fulfillment of this last requirement. That population is being built by the continuing redemption of those who willfully enter into a personal relationship with God based on the sacrificial death and the resurrection of Jesus Christ.

In God's perfect timing, the redemptive fix will be completed in two parts. The first part we have already reviewed – the eternal salvation of human beings who have entered into a personal relationship with God through Jesus Christ. The second part will be the final redemption of the fallen created order. At that time God will fashion a new heaven and new earth out of the ruins of the fallen creation. Then, God will put his resurrected people on this recreated paradise to once again dwell physically and personally with him for eternity. This what theologians call "glorification."

Eternity

In the beginning of this section, we noted that everything begins with an understanding of the purpose of God. Nothing in the

Christian faith makes sense until we understand why God did what he did in making his creation. Once we understand that, the culmination of God's plan is clear.

God's plan for the redemption of mankind is a process that began in the mind of God. It was put into effect at his instigation through the creation of the world and of mankind. The ultimate outworking of his plan is expressed in the life of each individual human being based on the decisions made during life on earth.

The first necessary step for an individual is to enter into the salvation process. In theological terms, this is called "justification." An individual makes a personal decision to repent of sin and accept God's forgiveness by inviting Jesus Christ into his or her life as Savior and Lord.

But salvation does not end there. In fact, that is only the first step in the process. The second step is referred to as "sanctification." This phase starts at the point of justification and continues for the rest of one's physical life. During this time, believers strive to live in an intimate relationship with God. This relationship is manifested through a process of spiritual maturation. God's plan is that the believer grow steadily more holy.

When an individual invites Christ into his or her life, God performs a miracle and creates a holy place within the individual's body – a place without sin. This is also often referred to as the new nature. God, in the form of the Holy Spirit, then takes up residence inside of that holy place within the believer. This is why Scripture sometimes calls the believer's body a "temple of the Holy Spirit" (see 1 Cor. 6:19). In that form, God enjoys fellowship with the individual believer. He also teaches him and manifests power to overcome the sin nature which still works to beat the individual down. It is the Christian's task to grow in that relationship by striving for holiness and fulfill the calling God has placed on his life. As the relationship becomes stronger, more and more sin is put aside and the salvation process begun at justification becomes more complete.

This brings us to the third and final step of the salvation process. This culminating aspect of God's redemptive plan is referred to as "glorification" and takes place at physical death.

As it turns out, when the believer receives the new nature, the old sin nature is still present. This is why the tendency to sin continues after justification. The old and new natures operate in conflict with one another during the time of the sanctification process.

At physical death, the old nature gets scraped off. Those who invited Christ into their lives during their physical life on earth will leave the physical body with its sin nature and enter directly into the presence of God. This begins the final phase of the salvation process in which the believer dwells with him for the rest of eternity.

This initial entry into heaven, however, is not the final step of God's redemptive plan. Redemption involves not only the salvation of the human person, but also the restoration of the created physical order corrupted by the introduction of sin. When the full number of believing human beings is accomplished according to God's plan, he will put an end to the sin corrupted created order and recreate it as a "new heaven and new earth." This will represent the restoration of God's original plan for eternal life.

At that point, all believers brought into the presence of God at their deaths will be physically resurrected to the new earth and given resurrected glorified bodies. We will inherit glorified heavenly bodies that, like Jesus' resurrected body, will have access to the spiritual realm of the new heaven and the physical new earth.

In this new condition, God will do what he originally did with Adam and Eve – he will dwell among us. At that point, all of the resurrected human beings will have direct access to God. We will experience him as a close friend as well as the Ruler of all creation. As was mentioned earlier as we discussed the creation, this does not limit God's ability to be God in all of eternity. But as a part of his plan, he will also manifest himself on the new earth.

In this new heaven and earth there will be no pain or sorrow or death. We will all do productive and purposeful work and will experience our eternal life as joyful and in no way monotonous or boring. It will be fulfilling and meaningful every moment of every day. It will truly be the ultimate expression of paradise. Believers will live eternally and experience the glory of God to the full extent that it is possible for each individual to do so.

A lot of details about the new heaven and new earth are not specifically revealed in Scripture. God has, though, shared with us the big picture. In the end, he will completely overcome the destructive attempt of Satan to disrupt his creation. The effects of sin will be overcome and the created order will emerge fully developed as God originally intended it. He will have his created world and a class of eternal Kingdom citizens who will personally interact and engage him in a mutually loving relationship throughout eternity.

4. Share the Content of the Gospel Message

All of the things dealt with up until now set the stage for sharing the message of the gospel. It is essential to build a bridge of understanding between the person who is hearing the gospel and the message itself. But setting the stage is meaningless unless we bring the person to a place where they can actually make a decision to enter into a personal relationship with God.

To do this, we must explain the content of the gospel message itself. The content of the gospel is contained in the essentials of the Christian faith. We have already discussed the concept of "the essentials" as it relates to worldview in general and to specific belief systems. It is the line that cannot be crossed and still remain within any given belief system. This line exists for the Christian faith, as well, and it is the explanation of this line that we must make clear as we share the gospel. The essentials are clarified as we answer four simple questions:

1) Who is God?
2) What is a human being?
3) What is salvation?
4) How does one achieve salvation?

The answers to these questions for the Christian faith are revealed in the Bible. As such, we answer the questions using Scripture. Many practical methods have been developed to share this knowledge. The various methods use different imagery to make the explanation. They may also use different Scripture verses. But regardless of how it is put together, the explanation must somehow answer these four questions.

Who Is God?

One of the first things we need to share is an explanation of the God of the Bible. In order to help an individual put their decision in context, there are certain things about God that we need to make sure they understand.

1. God is a person (Genesis 1:26-27),
2. God is holy (Psalm 97:1-2),
3. God is just (Deuteronomy 10:17-18), and
4. God is love (John 3:16).

These points are critical because they relate specifically to how God's being is connected to the salvation process.

It is important to recognize that God is a *person* because only persons are able to have self-conscious relationships. God created us as persons allowing us to fellowship with him as a person.

God's *holiness* (moral perfection) is important because it expresses why sin is such a problem. Our sin prevents us from interacting with God because he will not fellowship with sin.

Knowing God is *just* is critical because this expresses the consequences to our rebellion against him. When we sin, God will pronounce judgment against it. Judgment has eternal consequences when a person dies without having his or her sin forgiven.

Finally, God's *love* is critical because he cares enough for us to have provided a means of satisfying his justice. His love moved him to provide us a way to enter into a relationship with him. God's love is a constant, but he doesn't force it upon us. We have to love him back and express it by inviting Christ into our lives.

What Is a Human Being?

Two points concerning the nature of mankind must to be emphasized to make sure the person clearly understands God's purpose for humanity and our problem with sin.

1. We are made in God's image (Genesis 1:26-27), and
2. We are fallen creatures (Romans 3:23, Romans 5:12).

The fact that we are *made in the image of God* does not mean human beings physically look like God. Rather, we are the same quality of being as is he. This element allows us to interact with him in a personal relationship.

Understanding that we are *fallen creatures* is also critical. This fallenness permeates our human nature and inclines us to rebel against God. It does not mechanically make us rebel, but it does incline us in that direction. We are still creatures possessing a free will who can choose to rebel or not. That being the case, we are responsible for any rebellion we express. This rebellion puts us outside of a relationship with God and creates the necessity for salvation.

What Is Salvation?

The Bible reveals that God, as a Trinity, is a person who does not need another being to have his personal need for relationship fulfilled. As three persons in one, he completely satisfies that need within himself. But, for some reason, he wanted another personal being with whom he could express his love further. Mankind was created to fulfill that purpose.

Initially, things worked out fine. But, at a certain point, God's plan was interrupted by the introduction of sin into the world. Sin corrupted every element of God's creation including the physical universe. It also created a specific problem for mankind. Since God is holy and will not allow sin into his presence, the introduction of sin into the world separated the creation from God.

The first problem relates to how we live in this world (Romans 6:23). Mankind was corrupted in such a way as to prevent the personal interaction with God. That interaction was the purpose of mankind's existence in the first place. And before sin entered the world, man interacted with God in a personal relationship. This interaction occurred in God's perfect paradise – the Garden of Eden. But, with the entry of sin, mankind was tarnished in a way which prevents the relationship from occurring.

In God's economy this is not an unsolvable problem, but is beyond the reach of humanity's own ability. Mankind does not have the power within himself to remove the sin. In this life, human beings are not able to accomplish the purpose for which we were created. People have a constant and unfilled gap in their lives expressed by hatred, anger, jealousy, selfishness and so on. Mankind is in a hopeless situation unless some power from the outside accomplishes the fix.

Besides the gap people experience in their spiritual lives, they also think and behave in ways displeasing to God. These thoughts and actions have consequences in society. Not only is the relationship with God corrupt, but so are the relationships between human beings. This is expressed in broken homes, abused spouses and children, tension in the workplace, political upheaval and even war.

If the results of this problem were confined to this life, it would be bad enough. But, unfortunately, mankind's inability to fulfill God's purpose is not limited to life on earth. People are in danger of being separated from God throughout eternity (1 Corinthians 6:9-10; 2 Thessalonians 1:8-9). Since humans were created to be eternal spiritual beings, their essential personhood continues even after physical death with two possible destinies. They will spend eternity either in the presence of God or out of the presence of God. If they desire to live eternally in the presence of God, the sin problem must be resolved. God will not allow sin to exist in his presence. So without some kind of fix for the sin problem, mankind is lost and without hope for eternity.

So, just how is the sin problem solved? Since sin entered the world through the disobedience of a human being, it had to be defeated by the obedience of a human being. This obedience had the effect of reversing what was done at the Fall. According to the biblical revelation, a fix of this nature required some person to live a perfect life (without any sin), then die as a sacrificial substitute for those who failed to live up to God's holiness (John 3:16, Romans 8:10-11, Ephesians 2:1-6, John 1:12).

Those individuals who commit sin should have to pay for their own rebellion against God. This penalty for sin is death. But death, in this case, is not merely physical, it is spiritual death – eternal separation from God (Romans 6:23a).

Nonetheless, God created mankind for fellowship and was determined not to be defeated by Satan. So God instituted the fix. But in order to do so he could not use an ordinary human being. All ordinary humans start already immersed in sin. So, God needed a person who did not already have the sin nature within.

To provide the solution, God determined to come to earth himself and take the form of a human. He was born of a woman, but the father was not a human father. The Holy Spirit miraculously came upon the Virgin Mary to form a man who was not corrupted by sin. That person was Jesus Christ.

As Jesus lived on earth, he fulfilled all of the requirements necessary to qualify as the sacrifice for mankind's sins – that is, he lived a life totally free of sin. Then, having qualified to be the sacrifice, he died on the cross and actually became the sacrifice.

In this case, the sacrifice could not be the guilty person who should have to pay for his own sin. Rather, it had to be an innocent person who willingly sacrificed himself as a substitute. The theological term for this process is called *substitutionary atonement*. This doctrine says that sin had to be appeased by an innocent sacrifice, with the sacrificed person taking the place of the guilty party. Christ's resurrection from the dead validated the entire process. It showed that he indeed had the power and authority to carry out this task.

Christ's death on the cross and resurrection accomplished the fix that God determined to carry out. The power of sin was broken and mankind became qualified to have sin forgiven without personally paying the penalty.

How Does One Achieve Salvation?

The substitutionary sacrifice of Christ makes God's salvation applicable to the lives of individual human beings. But, just because this application is possible does not mean it is applied automatically. A requirement must be met – though not a requirement based on human effort. It is based on the grace of God (Ephesians 2:8-9) and received through the application of our faith in Jesus Christ (John 1:12). To receive this gift of eternal life, one must make a free-will decision to turn his or her life over to God and become his bond servant (Revelation 3:20). It is this act of receiving Christ and turning our lives over to him which causes the salvation, which God has provided, to be applied individually.

5. Lead the Person to a Decision

Once we have shared with an individual how they can know a personal relationship with God, the only thing left is for the person to actually make the decision to receive Christ. The fact that Christ died for mankind's salvation does not mean that it is automatically applied to individual's lives. We must make a personal, free-will decision to receive it.

Salvation is not merely an intellectual choice. Certainly no one can make the choice until it is intellectually understood, but the choice is not merely to believe with the mind. It actually requires that individuals entrust their lives into God's care. This means that they must be willing to live in his presence, obey his direction, and live a lifestyle reflecting God's character. It means putting aside selfish and sinful ways and willingly living according to his will.

When we lead a person to understand who God is, and he or she finally understands the salvation process, that individual is then in a position to make a choice whether or not to accept God's offer. At that point, we must be careful that we not attempt to make the person's choice for them. As much as we might desire a person to choose Christ, we cannot force them to do so. Ultimately, we are not responsible, in any way, for another person's decision. Our responsibility ends when we deliver the message. As a result, we do not get the credit when a person accepts Christ, nor the blame if they don't. This does not mean that we should no longer interact with the person. We should continue to try and help them in various ways regarding their spiritual walk. It is just that we are limited in what we can do by the decision they make.

As such, we need to view ourselves as facilitators who create an environment which allows us to make a gospel presentation and bring the other person to a point where they can make a decision concerning Christ. But, no matter what choice our friend makes, we must continue on in an open and viable relationship.

6. Follow Through

Sharing our faith is not a one-step deal. It is a process, and people have to first be brought to a place where they are willing to listen. We must then give the kind of information that allows our witness to make sense.

Once we have taken care of the matters mentioned above, we are ready to actually share our faith whenever the opportunities open up. This could happen at any time and we need to be prepared at all times.

Most of our sharing opportunities will not be one-shot presentations. One day we will talk about God, another day about morality, another day about the Bible and so on. The opportunity to really get down to cases may happen after a tragedy or when the person feels particularly isolated and lonely. Or it could be from some other life circumstance. But when the time comes, we have to be ready and willing.

If the Person Does Not Accept Christ

What if we share our faith with someone who decides not to accept Christ? Do we then just throw the relationship away? Of course not! If the person walks away, we may not have much say regarding how he goes forward. Hopefully the relationship is such that even a rejection of Christ does not destroy the mutual trust and respect that we have developed with our friend.

It may be that this individual does not yet understand all of the implications of receiving Christ. Or possibly he understands and is not yet willing to alter his lifestyle to the degree he knows is necessary. It may just be a matter of time for him to process the whole thing. People have all kinds of reasons not to accept Christ at any given moment. But if the relationship and mutual respect and trust stay in place, other opportunities down the road will come when we can share with them again.

If the Person Does Accept Christ

Suppose you present the gospel and the person does receive Christ. Is your work done? Absolutely not! Salvation is not simply a single moment in time. It is a process that works itself out throughout the rest of one's life. We receive Christ at a particular point in time, but the salvation process involves us growing in the image of Christ.

This process will not only involve learning what a life in Christ is like, but also the changing of old lifestyle habits. Changing one's lifestyle is a particularly difficult process for someone who has lived in ways contrary to God's way. Both learning and changing lifestyle habits are hard work. Typically, a new Christian needs a lot of encouragement and support – especially in the early stages. Jesus referred to the entry into relationship with God as being "born again." A new Christian is, literally, a spiritual baby, and babies cannot do much for themselves. They need a lot of help and support.

When we lead someone to Christ, we need to be there for them. The relationship we have with them puts us in that position and we ought to take it very seriously.

Sharing a Witness

As can be seen in this chapter, there are numerous elements we must master to be truly effective witnesses in every life circumstance.

The various people we interact with are all at different places in their understanding of the Christian message and in their personal readiness to receive it into their lives. We have to assess each person to figure out where they are and share specifically the knowledge that they need. If we master the principles in this chapter, we can share an effective and credible witness no matter the situation.

Chapter 7

Witness in Daily Life

"I just think we should let how we live our lives be our witness to unsaved people," remarked Jane as she sat in the women's Bible class. "I believe that when people see how we live they will want to know more about why Christianity is true. We can then tell them about Jesus."

"I think all we need to do is just tell everyone we can the simple gospel message," countered Sue. "Those who are meant to get saved will, and those who aren't intended to, won't. We just have to tell them!"

"There's something to be said for both of those ideas," replied Claire, the teacher. "So how many people have you two led to the Lord using your approaches?"

Jane and Sue looked at each other. Neither answered.

Whenever the topic of witness comes up, it often generates a discussion about whether it needs to be verbal or if just "living the life in front of people" is enough. This is a totally false dichotomy. A faithful witness involves both living it out and speaking it. It is like two sides of a single coin. We are not faithful witnesses if our lives don't demonstrate our faith, and we are not faithful witnesses if we do not share it.

The Great Commission in Matthew 28:18-20 is instructive at this point. It reads: *Then Jesus came to them and said, "All authority in heaven and on earth has been given to me. Therefore go and make disciples of all nations, baptizing them in the name of the Father and of the Son and of the Holy Spirit, and teaching them to obey everything I have commanded you. And surely I am with you always, to the very end of the age."* NIV The phrase, "Therefore go and make disciples of all nations" has a nuance in the Greek language not clearly evident in most English translations. It literally means, "As you are going, make disciples of all nations." This idea of "as you are going" is a reference to lifestyle, not about going to a particular location. Jesus is telling believers that we are to be faithful witnesses in every part of our lives no matter when and where we go.

To grasp this more fully, we have to remember that salvation is not simply something that happens to us at a single point in time. It is a process that begins at a particular moment, but continues throughout eternity. As it relates to witnessing, though, we are particularly interested in the time from salvation's beginning point to the end of our mortal lives.

When someone invites Christ into his or her life, that person has stepped out of eternal death and into eternal life. That eternal life is not something picked up after we die, it begins when we receive salvation. As such, we are to live as those spiritually alive rather than those spiritually dead.

Of course, this does not mean we never sin again. As long as we still have the sin nature, we will struggle with that problem. Nonetheless, when Christ entered our lives we were given a new nature which makes it possible to overcome sin. Our whole life after the moment of salvation is to be devoted to living for Christ.

This plays out two ways as it relates to our witness. The first concerns "faithful living." A true believer is going to live a life that reflects Christ as the master. The second way involves faithful verbal sharing. A person who truly knows Christ will not be ashamed to speak about him.

As we saw above, in the Great Commission, God calls every believer to partner with him in spreading the gospel. The very reason we exist, and why God created mankind in the first place, was for fellowship with himself. As such, our lives should focus on *his* purpose. This involves being in position to fellowship with him (putting aside sin) and sharing with others how they can know him (witness).

Learning how to share our faith with other people is not an option. Sure, it takes work and practice to learn the information and become skilled at sharing it. The only obstacle, though, is a decision not to do it. Once we decide we will, we can do it. The information is available. In fact, that is what this whole book has been about.

Possible Contexts for Sharing a Witness

There are several possible approaches to physically interacting with people to share a witness. Each approach has its place and it is important to be aware of them so that we can be used by God appropriately.

1. Cold Call Witnessing

Cold call witnessing is the method most promoted in modern witness training programs. Most training programs don't expressly advocate cold calling, but they often end up promoting that approach by default. The reason is that most training programs only focus on how to share the gospel message per se (building the gospel bridge), and not with the context of the witness (building a worldview bridge). As such, people are taught to share the gospel and then told, "Now go out and do it."

Certainly this approach is not a bad thing. There are times when is appropriate, such as in neighborhood canvassing situations or in special evangelistic events like street witnessing.

But those kinds of cold call approaches do not fit everyone equally. God has specifically called and gifted some people to be effective with this kind of witnessing and these people ought to be faithful to their calling.

Other Christians don't have that gift. But even they are not off the hook. Every believer needs to be equipped to give a witness when the opportunity presents itself. Sometimes we just come across a person who is ready to receive the gospel. We may meet someone at work or when visit in a home who asks how to know God. At the very least we ought to be able to share that information.

We also must be careful about one other thing when doing cold call witnessing. It is very easy to become impersonal in this process. The focus can easily change from leading the individual to God to getting notches on our gun. Witnessing is about leading people into relationship with God, not about how many people we can get to "pray the prayer."

So, cold call witnessing has its place. Every believer ought to be able to do it if the circumstances are right. But it needs to be used in a proper context to be effective.

2. Relationships

The truth is, cold call witness is only effective for sharing with certain kinds of people – those who are ready, at that moment, to step into a life with Christ. However, the large majority of non-believers we interact with are not at that point. Many don't understand the meaning of the message or still have a rebellious heart. Because of that, in most situations, we need a way to share a witness with people over a longer period of time. Long-term relationships are the key to this process.

Research has shown that most people who come to Christ do so by the influence of friends and family – not on the basis of a cold call encounter. As such, it is critical for every believer to live a faithful life among his or her relationships, both by lifestyle and words.

In the case of relationships, a call and a gift are not necessary. Every believer is commissioned by God to be a faithful witness, even those without the specific calling and gifting of an evangelist. All Christians need to pay attention to the non-believers in their web of relationships and look for opportunities to share Christ.

3. Going out on Mission

Going out on mission is another possibility for witness. In this case, we may use either of the above approaches. The focus here is more on the location of the witness than the methodology used when sharing the message.

Mission opportunities in our day have radically expanded because of advances in communication and transportation technology. It used to be that missionary work required lots of time and money and was pretty much left up to the "professional." But in the day in which we live, there is a place for both long term and short term missions. Both of these options are available for the so called professional as well as the non-professional.

Mission possibilities abound both inside and outside of one's own country. It is not difficult, now, to get involved in missionary work. All kinds of groups facilitate short term mission work making it possible for average church members to participate in a host of activities. And for those led to missions as a career, numerous denominational and parachurch groups serve as sending agencies. In any case, the full range of witnessing skills are essential, including an understanding of worldview and a knowledge of the gospel message.

Focus on Worldview Thinking

As we have seen, effective witness involves more than merely sharing the message of the gospel. Of course, the gospel message must be in the mix and it is necessary that, at some point, every individual have the opportunity to make a decision concerning what they will do with Christ.

Nonetheless, the witness also involves putting the gospel message in a form that makes sense to the listener. We must understand what the other person believes and frame the presentation to bridge the gap between what they believe and the truth about salvation.

As Christians, it is time to up our game. We have to become better. We have to expand our knowledge. We have to be more skilled in every part of the witnessing process. This is not that difficult since the things we need to know are readily available. But we don't get it just by sitting back and letting our faith life just "happen." We have to take some initiative. And when we do, God will use us to touch the lives of people in profound ways to lead them into an intimate relationship with him.

Part IV - Resources for Effective Witness

Witnessing Resource 1 - Overview of Various Belief Systems
Witnessing Resource 2 - Breakdown of Popular Witnessing Methods
Witnessing Resource 3 - The Seven Worldview Questions
Witnessing Resource 4 - Witnessing Issues in Cross-cultural Missions

Witnessing Resource 1
Overview of Various Belief Systems

Explanation of the Major Naturalistic Groups 105
    Secular Humanism 106
    Postmodernism 109
    Atheism/Agnosticism 112
    Marxism 115

Explanation of the Major Animistic Groups 119
    Wicca/Neo-paganism 120
    Shinto 123
    Voodoo/Santeria 126
    Native American Religions 129
    Non-American Tribal Religions 131

Explanation of the Major Far Eastern Thought Groups . 133
    Hinduism 134
    Buddhism 137
    Hare Krishna 140
    Sikhism 143

Explanation of the Major non-Christian Theistic Groups 147
    Islam 148
    Judaism 151
    Cultural Christianity 154
    Jehovah's Witnesses 157
    Mormonism 160
    Baha'I 163

Explanation of the Major Hybrid Groups 167
    New Age 168
    Unitarian Universalism 171
    Scientology 174
    Christian Science 177
    Unification Church 180

Explanation of the Major Naturalistic Groups

Secular Humanism
Postmodernism
Atheism/Agnosticism
Marxism

Secular Humanism

"Humanism" in and of itself is not necessarily bad or anti-God. It simply emphasizes the importance and value of mankind. Secular Humanism, on the other hand, is a coherent dogmatic system which believes there is no such thing as a supernatural existence. It asserts that since man is the only known creature with personal self-awareness, he only can create values and standards. Thus, man is the ultimate standard by which all of life is measured and judged.

Background

Modern Secular Humanism began during the Renaissance in the 14th to 17th centuries. This early incarnation did not exclude God as man's creator, but did focus attention away from him. Later, the development of modern science advanced humanist ideas. Along with that, 18th century Deism affirmed belief in a God no longer active in creation or as Father to mankind.

In the 19th century, Deism gave way to Naturalism which threw God out altogether. Elements of humanist philosophy even crept into mainline Christian churches. The trend peaked with Charles Darwin's (1809 - 1882) book, *On the Origin of Species*, which asserted that humanity's origin was completely natural.

In the 20th century, scientists, philosophers, and liberal theologians promoted humanism as a non-theistic religion devoid of the supernatural. Unitarianism, once a non-Trinitarian sect of Christianity, fully adopted the concepts of Humanism. In 1933, the Humanist Manifesto I was drafted as a creed of humanist thought. But Secular Humanism's optimism for perfecting human society was shattered by World War II and its aftermath. Nonetheless, many diehards continued to proclaim its tenets.

In 1973, the Humanist Manifesto II was released. In 2003, they updated it in the Humanist Manifesto III. Today, Secular Humanism dominates public educational and political institutions, as well as the news media and the entertainment industry.

Basic Beliefs and Practices

The Secular Humanist Manifesto III is more of a consensus statement than the previous documents, but disavows none of what they said.

Its main points are:
- Knowledge is derived by observation, experimentation, and rational analysis.
- Humans are part of nature, the result of unguided evolutionary change.
- Ethical values derive from human experience.
- Life's fulfillment is found serving humane ideals.
- Humans find meaning in relationships.
- Working to benefit society maximizes individual happiness.

These points attract idealistic people, but one must read the entire manifesto to fully understand what it entails. Manifestos I and II provided clearer perspectives than the generic points of the current manifesto. They asserted such concepts as:
- Promises of immortal salvation or fear of eternal damnation are illusory and harmful.
- Moral values come from human experience.
- Reason and intelligence are the most effective instruments of humankind.
- The dignity of the individual is the central value.
- Intolerant attitudes unduly repress sexual conduct. The right to birth control, abortion, and divorce should be recognized.
- The individual must experience a full range of civil liberties in all societies. These include freedom of speech, press, democracy, opposition to government policies, fair judicial process, religion, association, artistic expression, science, culture, death with dignity, euthanasia and suicide.
- Society should be open and democratic.
- Separation of church or ideology and state.
- Equality must be furthered by elimination of all discrimination based upon race, religion, sex, age or national origin.
- Mankind's division on nationalistic grounds is deplorable.
- The world community must renounce violence and force for solving international disputes.
- The world community must engage in cooperative planning for managing depleting resources.
- The problems of economic development are worldwide in scope and the developed nations must equalize the distribution of resources.

- We resist any moves to censor scientific research on moral, political or social grounds.
- All travel restrictions must cease and the world be open to diverse political, ideological and moral viewpoints.

Essential Beliefs
God
There is no type of supernatural existence at all (God, gods, angels, ghosts, or any other kind of spiritual entity). Essentially, mankind is his own god. All that exists is eternal and evolving matter.

Man
Man is a biological machine resulting from Naturalistic evolution. Man has no life but what is experienced in this natural world, and is responsible for his own destiny.

Salvation
Salvation consists of fulfilling one's highest potential in mortal life. There is no life after death.

Postmodernism

Background

Postmodernism developed in the last century as a reaction against modernism and is difficult to define. It denies absolute truth and denounces Western philosophy. It also rejects universal or transcendent truth, yet endorses "political correctness." It is expressed in art, architecture, music, film, literature, and so on. No individual is identified as its "Father."

Postmodernists maintain that no objective right and wrong exists. They dismiss the fundamental ideas of all belief systems which they call "metanarratives." For instance, an American metanarrative is that democracy is the best form of government.

Postmodernism asserts that cultures are built on these metanarratives including science, art, architecture, music, technology, religion, etc. It insists that no metanarrative is any more viable than any other. Each view may be right for its own situation and context, but not necessarily for others.

Postmodernists, conversely, operate out of "mini-narratives." These focus on individual events rather than universal principles. Judgments are determined by the particular situation, with no objective right or wrong. What is right at one point may not be right at another. What is right for one person may not be right for another. No universal truth or morality is acknowledged. Thus, knowledge has a strictly functional influence on people's lives.

Basic Beliefs and Practices

Postmodernism is difficult to define because it denies absolute truth. The easiest way is to compare it with Modernism.

Education

Modernism: Objective truth exists to be transmitted to students.
Postmodernism: No objective truth exists. Teachers facilitate students to construct their own subjective ideas.

Health Care

Modernism: The body is studied by the scientific method. Medicine devises therapies.

Postmodernism: Alternative techniques without scientific confirmation are valid.

Science
Modernism: Universal laws of science are applied to the material world to solve problems.
Postmodernism: The universe is not based on absolute laws. The universe is interconnected but not rational.

Psychotherapy
Modernism: Mental health is defined objectively. Trained therapists help patients toward a healthy state of mind.
Postmodernism: The "right" mental state cannot be defined objectively. Therapists help patients construct what is right for themselves.

Religion
Modernism: Individuals can learn objective truths about God.
Postmodernism: No single religious perspective is correct. All exclusivist religious claims are denounced as "intolerant."

History
Modernism: History is an objective reality. Individuals can study events from the past.
Postmodernism: History is not objective. Studying past events is pointless except to validate oppressed people's protests of society.

Literature
Modernism: Ideas flow from an author to a reader through the written word. An author produces a text which objectively communicates propositions to the reader.
Postmodernism: Meaning flows from the *reader*, not the author. Individuals construct subjective meaning filtered through their own cultural framework.

Biblical Interpretation
Modernism: Scripture is propositional truth delivered from God through divinely inspired authors. Interpretation is the process of

discerning the truth God conveys by legitimate methods (hermeneutics).
Postmodernism: God does not communicate truth through the Bible. It is simply another book from which readers extract subjective meaning filtered through their own culture.

Law and Government
Modernism: Laws are objective principles established to keep order in society. In a democratic republic, judges discern the intent of the writers and interpret them.
Postmodernism: All laws are political constructs designed to suppress the disenfranchised. Judges cannot objectively interpret the intent of laws but pursue their own personal political agendas.

Morality
Modernism: Right morality can be extrapolated from objective truth.
Postmodernism: Right and wrong is "what is moral for the individual." Most Postmodernists, nonetheless, would add ... "as long as it doesn't hurt anyone."

Essential Beliefs
Postmodernists incongruently deny objective truth but cannot live by that assertion. They must draw a line defining the parameters of reality that, as with all worldview positions, cannot be crossed and still be Postmodern. The essential elements of Postmodernism include:

God
The concept of God is determined by each individual. No transcendent God created a meaningful world.

Man
Human beings are animal creatures and no different from any other except for the evolutionary development of the brain. They are not spiritual beings but must find their own personal meaning for life.

Salvation
Postmodernist "salvation" is finding personal meaning in a universe with no transcendent meaning.

Atheism, Agnosticism and Skepticism

Background

Here we want to look at not only Atheism, but Agnosticism and Skepticism, as well. The three positions have distinct differences but pretty much land in the same place. All three of these views are firmly in the camp of Naturalism. It is often difficult to distinguish between the terms because their definitions overlap. Many people who label themselves with one of these expressions do not see the differences or how their own views fit one category or the other. We will try to make a distinction between the three beliefs as well as stress where they intersect.

Because of the nature of these philosophical points of view, no distinctive history is identified with them. These positions have been held by people over the centuries.

Atheism

The word Atheism literally means "without god." It derives from the Greek prefix *a* meaning "not" or "without," and *theos* meaning "God." Thus, an Atheist believes there is no such thing as God (gods). They assert that all of existence can be explained naturally.

Agnosticism

The word Agnosticism also comes from the Greek. It combines the Greek *a* with the word *gnosis* (knowledge). Thus, it literally means "without knowledge." Agnostics maintain there is not enough evidence to prove or disprove the existence of God. A true agnostic criticizes both the Theist and the Atheist for presuming to have such knowledge. This position attempts to remain neutral on the topic of God by suspending judgment.

Agnosticism has two primary expressions. One asserts there is not enough evidence to know if there is a God, but leaves open the possibility of obtaining that knowledge. The second type asserts that it is impossible to ever know with certainty whether or not God exists.

Skepticism

The word Skepticism is derived from the Greek word *skeptomai* meaning "to doubt" or "to consider." Skeptics believe that people cannot know truth with absolute certainty, so they should suspend judgment about it. Their skepticism applies not only to knowledge of God, but to all truth claims.

Basic Beliefs and Practices

Though the three approaches to denying God are semantically different, their practical consequences are the same. They all deny God, but argue this denial differently. Some of the more common arguments include:

The Language Argument

The Language Argument asserts that only two kinds statements are meaningful: 1) pure definition; and 2) what can be empirically verified. Since God cannot be defined or empirically verified, it is meaningless to talk about him.

The Knowledge Argument

The Knowledge Argument denies that we can objectively know what is real because our senses are imperfect. We can only know what we experience, albeit imperfectly.

The Moral Concepts Argument

The Moral Concepts Argument asserts that if there is a good, all-powerful God, he would not allow evil to exist. So, since evil exists, God does not.

The Scientific Methods Argument

The Scientific Methods Argument is psychological and related to man's feelings. Since human beings are not able to deal with all life's struggles, they feel an inner need to be rescued. Since they assume that there is no transcendent God, belief in God can only arise from man's wish for someone powerful enough to be the rescuer.

The Logic Arguments

Nay-sayers sometimes posit a couple of fallacious logical arguments in their attempt to deny the existence of God.

1. One argument is to say God's all-powerfulness is contradictory. This group asserts that if God is all-powerful, he could reconcile any contradiction (eg., God could make a square circle.) Since he can't do so, he must not exist.

2. A second argument is that God's attributes are contradictory. For instance, how can he be both love and wrath at the same time?

Essential Beliefs
God
Atheists, Agnostics and Skeptics all assert that there is no such thing as God, or at least there is no possibility that we can know.

Man
Atheists, Agnostics and Skeptics all affirm that man is the chance result of billions of years of natural evolutionary progress.

Salvation
Atheists, Agnostics and Skeptics all assert that there is no life after death, so achieving maximum fulfillment in this life is mankind's highest aim.

Marxism

Background

Marxism is an economic and political philosophy named for Karl Marx. It is also known as scientific socialism. Marxism has had a profound impact on contemporary culture. Most modern socialist theories have originated from it.

Karl Marx was born in Trier, Germany in 1818. His ancestors were Jewish rabbis. Prior to his birth, around 1816, his father, Heinrich, converted to Christianity in order to continue practicing law. He did this because the Prussian government had passed a law denying Jews the opportunity to serve in this profession. His mother converted when Karl was seven.

In daily life, the family did not demonstrate much interest in religion, but his parents raised Karl in an atmosphere of religious toleration. He even attended a religious school, though the purpose was for a superior academic education rather than for religious training.

For his higher education, Marx attended Bonn University. He later worked on his doctorate at Berlin University. During that time, he became a committed Atheist and a political and social radical. His views were so radical that he was unable to get a job as a professor, so he turned his focus to political activism. In order to share his ideas with a wider audience, he became the editor of a business periodical which also had a bent toward radical political viewpoints. In that position, he was able to more fully develop and express his philosophy of dialectical materialism.

In 1843 he met Frederich Engles who became a close friend, benefactor and collaborator. They were very much philosophical and political soul-mates. That same year, because of Marx's radical activism, the German government closed his publication and expelled him from Germany. From there he moved to Paris.

Not too long after that, his radical activism got him in trouble again and he was kicked out of France. From there he moved to Brussels, Belgium where, in 1948, Marx and Engles wrote the *Communist Manifesto*.

Following its publication he was expelled from Belgium and he attempted to go back to Germany. They would not let him stay there, so he tried, once again, to move to France. But they also would not let him return, so he moved to London. Because of his devotion to his cause, he basically lived a paupers life. He was often reduced to begging money from friends and relatives to pay his debts. He finally achieved some measure of financial success and stability after publishing *Das Kapital* in 1867. He died in 1883.

Basic Beliefs and Practices

Marxism is not just a political and economic philosophy, it is a comprehensive belief system. As such, it affirms an atheistic religious viewpoint and a contempt for philosophy. Although no single writing by Marx covers all aspects of Marxism, the *Communist Manifesto* and *Das Kapital* develop his ideas most completely.

The core of Marxism is expressed in the concept of dialectical materialism. This philosophy asserts that economic factors are the primary determinants of the flow of history. From this foundation, Marx developed the basic thesis that the history of society is actually the history of class struggle.

According to his assumptions, a specific class could only stay in power as long as it was the best representative of the most economically productive group in society. When it could no longer maintain that status, it would be destroyed and replaced. He believed that through this process a classless society would eventually emerge.

According to Marx's theory, the capitalist society of his day had destroyed the unproductive feudal nobility which went before, and had replaced it with a new industrial order. In his mind, the stage was set for one final struggle between the capitalist class (bourgeoisie), which had completed its historic role, and the working class (proletariat) who had become the new productive class. He believed that it was these industrial workers who would complete the revolution by overturning capitalism and create a true classless society.

Essential Beliefs
God

The Marxist god is humanity's inevitable march toward societal perfection based on dialectical materialism. This belief is built on the understanding that there is no God, but that mankind is master of his own destiny.

Man

Marxism denies the worth and freedom of the individual. Individuals have value only as they promote the common good of society.

Salvation

Salvation is achieved as individuals deny their own personal desires and find the place where they can most effectively contribute to the collective society.

Explanation of the Major Animistic Groups

Wicca/Neo-paganism
Shinto
Voodoo/Santeria
Native American Religions
Non-American Tribal Religions

Wicca/Neo-paganism

Background

Wicca is a particular expression of Animism out of the broader witchcraft tradition. Many groups claim that title with differing uses of magic, rituals, religious practice, and views of the spirit world. All encompass worship and practice that includes magic and rituals to influence the spirit world.

Witchcraft can be traced back many centuries in Africa, Europe and the Middle East. It has no personal understanding of God. Rather, divine beings are seen to inhabit nature. The natural order is sometimes personified as a god or goddess, but not in a personal way.

Derivatives of ancient witchcraft are still practiced throughout the world. The most common modern form was started in 1949 by an English eccentric named Gerald Gardner (1884 - 1964). His book, *The Craft*, used the word "Wicca" as a form of nature worship where the spirit world is present in the natural order. His inspiration was the pre-Christian pagan religions of Europe.

Gardner was fascinated with the occult. It is not clear if he intended to begin a new religious tradition, but it does seem that he invented this cult to satisfy his desire to explore occult ideas.

Witchcraft has been in America since its early days. Its greatest growth, however, took place in the 1960s and 1970s during a revival of interest in the occult. Two of Gardner's followers, Raymond and Rosemary Buckland, came to America in 1962 and established a Wiccan group (or coven) in Long Island, New York.

In 1973, a convention of Witches was held in Minneapolis, Minnesota, attracting 73 different groups. They attempted to write a unified statement of principles but failed because they could not agree on wording. The following year the Council of American Witches successfully drafted the "Covenant of the Goddess."

Basic Beliefs and Practices

The theology of Wicca varies from group to group. However, the following are a few of the doctrines common to most Wiccan covens.

- *Autonomy* - There is no central authority or liturgy. Each tradition (each local group of Wiccans) establishes its own

rituals, philosophy and beliefs. Individuals may also create their own.
- **Rituals** - Individual or coven experiences are manifested through self-designed rituals. Rites acknowledge the movement of the seasons and celebrate life processes.
- **Experience vs. Dogma** - The experience of the individual is of greater importance than any set of authoritarian doctrines.
- **Magic** - Rituals in Wicca involve divination or magic. This involves contacting and manipulating people, spirits, animals, plants, or the elements (earth, air, fire, water). It is done through occult rituals, ceremonies, or the use of magic objects (amulets, talismans, charms, etc.).
- **Goddess Worship** - Worship involves veneration of the "Mother Goddess" (Mother Nature). In many covens the high priestess is seen as the embodiment of the "Mother Goddess."
- **Feminism** - Many women find Wicca compatible with feminist thought since it focuses on a goddess.
- **Seasonal Festivals** - The worship of nature, or the natural order, is of chief importance. It is a fertility cult with festivals tied to the seasons.
- **Evil** - Wiccans deny the existence of evil. They consider themselves practitioners of a pagan mystery religion with no embodiment of evil such as Satan or the Devil.
- **Horned God** - Some covens worship a masculine deity along with the Goddess. This God is referred to as the Horned God, the God of the Hunt, the God of Death or the Lord of the Forests.

Essential Beliefs
God
Wicca has no personal God who is Creator and Sustainer of the universe. Rather, the divine life source in nature is open to contact through psychic power, mysticism or natural magic. This life source is present in everything. Many Wiccans worship the Great Goddess and the Horned God as focus objects rather than as personal deities.

Man
Human beings are natural creatures inhabiting the material world that can interact with the nature spirits to accomplish desired ends.

Salvation

Human beings have no need of salvation from sin. Some believe that at death the spirit of an individual enters the spirit world. Others believe in reincarnation. In any case, it is all connected with the natural order of the universe.

Worldview Resources

Shinto

History

Shinto is the indigenous religion of Japan. Essentially, it is a primitive religion which centers on the worship of nature deities and deified people. It has no founder, no prophet, no savior, and little formal doctrine. Its main emphasis is the worship of the Kami (gods). Kami are everywhere and the world is Kami.

The origins of the ancient Shinto religion are obscure. The word itself literally means "the way of the gods." The religion did not even have a name until the 6th century A.D. when it was named in order to distinguish it from Buddhism which had been imported from China. The early development of Shintoism is not recorded. Records only started being kept when Buddhism began to threaten Shintoism and the Japanese began writing things down as a way of preserving the old myths and oral traditions.

The Japanese usually have their wedding ceremonies in Shinto style and pronounce their wedding vows to Kami.

Basic Beliefs and Practices
The Creation Story

The origins of Shinto are recorded in the *Kojiki* and the *Nihongi*. According to the creation myth, after the formation of heaven and earth, two of the gods, Izanagi and Izanami, stood on the floating bridge of heaven. Izanagi was leisurely stirring the ocean brine with his spear, and when he lifted it out, the drops which fell from it coagulated to form one of the Japanese islands. Izanagi and Izanami descended to this island and produced the rest of the Japanese islands. They also produced other deities and the Japanese people.

One of the chief deities was the sun goddess, Amaterasu Omikami. She had a grandson named Jimmu Tenno who descended to the sacred Japanese islands to become the first historical emperor of Japan in 660 B.C. Japanese tradition claims an unbroken line of succession from Jimmu Tenno, and this has led to a strong emphasis on emperor worship. Since the emperors were thought to be gods, they had to be obeyed unquestioningly by all Japanese.

Nationalistic Shinto

Popular Shinto has no ethical system of its own, so ethical teachings from Confucianism and Buddhism were introduced. This is especially evident in the concepts of filial piety and the five relationships.

However, in the mid to late 1800s, a rise in Japanese nationalistic spirit led to a revival of popular Shinto at the expense of Buddhism. In 1882, Emperor Meiji officially made Shinto the state religion. State Shinto ultimately became a political force that was used to promote the superiority of the Japanese people and to prove that the creation of the Japanese Empire was a divine event. To solidify this movement, national Shinto shrines were established.

Before and during WWII, all students were indoctrinated in the Shinto myths and taught to worship the emperor and the state. In that way, the politicians were able to use State Shinto as the basis for their war effort. Thus, at the end of World War II, in 1946, when Emperor Hirohito denied that we was divine, it was a huge blow to the Shinto religion. Even though state Shinto was officially eliminated, there is still a core of nationalists who continue to promote it.

Essential Beliefs
God

There are many gods and even different types of gods. There are gods of nature, the ancestors, and the emperor. The emperor is a living human being while the other gods inhabit the spirit world. Even these, though, interact with humanity in a symbiotic relationship.

Man

Shinto teaches that "man is Kami's child." First, this means that a person was given his life by Kami, so his nature is sacred. Second, it means that daily life is made possible by the Kami, so human personality and life are worthy of respect. Man is considered to have a divine nature, but it is seldom revealed in this life. Purification ceremonies are necessary to symbolically remove the dust and impurities that cover one's inner mind.

Salvation

Salvation is achieved by observing the many social and physical taboos which have become a part of Japanese life. Ritualistic purity (ceremonial washing and sweeping) is very important since this is how evil is thought to be banished. The concept of salvation is deliverance from the troubles and evils of the world. There is no concept of sin in a biblical sense. If a person appeases the gods and ancestors, follows the correct taboos, and expresses his Kami nature, he will ultimately find his place of immortality among the ancestral Kami beings.

Voodoo/Santeria

Background

The first thing in most people's minds when thinking of Voodoo are of zombies walking around with their arms sticking out. They also think of witch doctors and sticking pins in dolls. The fact is, Voodoo is an Animistic religion with origins 6000 years ago in West Africa. The word Voodoo is from the Nigerian word vodu, meaning divinity, spirit or deity. The religion is also known as voudou, voudoun, vodoun, and hoodoo.

Voodoo's roots in the Western Hemisphere are from Haiti. Slaves from Africa were brought to the West Indies by Western Europeans. Those slaves were forced to convert to Roman Catholicism. However they did not completely assimilate into it. The result was a blend of Roman Catholic teachings with traditional African rituals.

Modern forms of Voodoo reflect this mixture. Ceremonies integrate Catholic rituals, prayers, liturgies, and reverence for the saints with old African Animistic observances. Voodoo worship places are often filled with pictures and statues of Catholic saints, and worship practices include hymns to the saints and the Virgin Mary. The saints may actually represent Voodoo gods.

Many slaves were sent from Haiti to what is now the United States. As a result, their descendants, and other adherents of Voodoo, still remain. Probably the best known enclave is New Orleans. Voodoo is also practiced in parts of South America, Africa, Trinidad, Jamaica, and Cuba.

Another similar, African originated, faith popular among many Cuban Americans is Santeria. The basics of Voodoo and Santeria are similar, though they differ in worship practices and how they identify the gods. Followers of Santeria, called Santeros, worship a number of gods including Obatalá, Oshún, Yemaya (or Yemallá), Oyá, Changó (or Shango), Elegguá, Oggún, Ochosi, and Osun. These are also often identified with Catholic saints. The supreme god is Olofi, also called Olodumare and Olorún. Santeros believe that ritually honoring and sacrificing small animals to these gods gains magical power to influence other people.

Basic Beliefs and Practices

Voodoo's basic tenet (and Santeria's, as well) is that entities in the spirit world interact with humans on earth in symbiotic relationships. Humans provide food and other materials to help the spirits. The spirits provide health, protection from evil and good fortune to humans. The entities are mixtures of ancestral spirits and lesser gods known as Loa. They interact in ritual ceremonies led by Voodoo priests or priestesses.

The rituals invoke the spirit's help. Various ceremonies celebrate lucky events or holidays, invoke help for escaping bad fortune, ask for healing, celebrate the birth of a child, bless a marriage, or provide a smooth transition into the afterlife at death.

Regional variations exist in Voodoo ceremonies, but they are basically similar. A priest or priestess presides with singing and dancing. Drum beats invoke the presence of the spirits as food and animal blood is offered. As the music, drink, and dance take effect, the priest, or someone else, falls into a trance as the Loa take possession of their body. In this state, a spirit may manifest itself by speaking, singing, cursing, offering advice or healing the sick.

Essential Beliefs
God

The one supreme god is named Bondje. Beneath Bondje, are hundreds of minor gods and Loa who are the spirits of departed people who led exceptional lives while on earth (much like saints in the Roman Catholic tradition). The Loa exercise control over nature and the health, wealth, and happiness of humans. Jesus Christ was not part of Voodoo tradition, but as Christian ideas mixed in, Jesus became one of their pantheon of gods.

Man

Human beings are material expressions of the universal life energy that all living things share. The physical body contains a soul with two parts. The "small soul" is an individual's personal essence. This part journeys out of the body during sleep (in dreams) and is possessed by the Loa during Voodoo ceremonies. The "large soul" is the universal life energy which enters an individual at conception and departs at death.

Salvation

Salvation does not concern forgiveness or overcoming sin. Rather, it addresses practical ways to make it through life. The gods help one navigate this life and to move smoothly into the next.

Worldview Resources

Native American Religions

Background

Explaining the worldview beliefs of Native American religions is more difficult than other belief systems because the large number of Native American tribes differ somewhat in their approaches. That being said, they all fall under the same worldview category. Our purpose here is not to explain each group's beliefs, but to analyze the worldview foundation of all traditional Native American religions.

Most Native American people groups were thought to have migrated to the Western Hemisphere from Siberia across the Bering Strait and spread throughout the Americas. Recent archeological discoveries, however, indicate that some migrations may have come from other areas.

Native American worship practices evolved differently because of tribal diversity and geographical distribution. Rituals emerged in each location reflecting individual situations. Some groups were oriented toward hunting and gathering and looked to the spirits to help them find game. Others were agricultural and depended on the spirits to provide weather that allowed for good crops. All, though, were founded on an Animistic worldview and held many things in common.

Modern Native American religious practices were influence by the arrival, in the 15th and 16th centuries, of Western Europeans to the Americas. As the new arrivals from Europe spread, every element of Native American life was altered. Many died due to illness and war. In some cases, Native American spiritual practices were suppressed and the populations forced to convert to Christianity. Also, government policies forced tribes onto reservations or compelled their assimilation into Western culture.

Because of this upheaval, Native Americans now follow a variety of spiritual traditions. Some are devout Christians while others maintain their traditional religions. It is also common to find ancient traditions syncretized with Christian or even New Age beliefs.

Basic Beliefs and Practices

While we recognize great diversity in the various Native American religious traditions, they nonetheless share several worldview similarities.

First, in every case, all of creation is seen to be interrelated and humans are responsible to oversee and protect the material world.

Second, all life is of equal value. A sacred life force is in all humans, animals and plants which connects all living things. All life forms have as much right to existence as human beings and should not be damaged or destroyed. Plants and animals may be used for food, medicine and other needs, but with limitations.

Third is a long term concern for life. They willingly forego short-term expediency to assure long-term viability in nature.

Finally, they express gratitude to the Creator for life and all he makes possible. This gratitude is expressed in public and private worship traditions.

The Native American view of deity is dualistic with good and bad in the spiritual world. Most believe in a creator God who made the world. They acknowledge him in worship and prayer. They also believe in other spirits which control the weather and other circumstances affecting humans.

Since Westerners entered the picture, Christianity has greatly penetrated Native American spirituality. Some New Age teachers have also incorporated Native American concepts into their principles, and vice versa. One such prominent New Age author was Sun Bear (born Vincent LaDuke, 1929 - 1992).

Essential Beliefs
God

Most Native American groups acknowledge an all-powerful, all-knowing creator God or "Master Spirit." They also recognize numerous lesser supernatural spirits which interact with material life from the spirit world.

Man

Mankind is one expression of the universal life force that courses through all living things. Man is to live harmoniously in the world and with all other living things, helping to maintain the web of life.

Salvation

Salvation does not concern the forgiveness of sin, rather with how to make it through this life. The spirits help people navigate the material world and move smoothly into the next.

Non-American Tribal Religions

Background

Native American religions are one category of Animistic peoples. Basically, they are tribal groups which existed in what is now the United States, before Europeans colonized that area of the world. While each of them have an Animistic foundation, the specific gods and religious practices vary considerably.

This type of religious practice is not, however, limited to the Americas. Tribal religions are found, literally, all over the world. The highest concentration of people who follow tribal religions in modern times are found in Africa. In some African countries, as many as 40-45% of the people follow some form of tribal religion. There is also a very high concentration of people who follow tribal religions in Mongolia and Laos. But even developed nations tend to have measurable groups which can be characterized as believers in a tribal religion.

Categories of tribal religions include groups which are identified by their ethnicity, groups which are organized around a shaman, and groups in which the animistic practices themselves are the chief identifier. In all cases, though, Animism is the approach they use for understanding the nature of reality. It is estimated that about 3% of the world's population fit into this category.

Basic Beliefs and Practices

Each tribal group tends to be unique when it comes to the specific gods worshiped and the practices used in worship. That being said, the similarities are also noticeable. Generally there is a belief in a cosmos populated by gods. This often includes a chief god which creates other gods, the earth, the animals, and human beings.

In the practice of these religions, there will usually be sacred places that a god or sacred spirit inhabits. It is also not unusual that both males and females are considered to be part of the cosmic scheme. This element of the belief system is often associated with fertility rites. In Animistic tribal groups, the religion is also generally the organizing principle for the operation of society, including its values and traditions.

The actual religious beliefs themselves tend not to have specific tenets with religious laws to follow. The emphasis is generally on making sure that the spirit world and the physical world are properly related and that the needs of each side are taken care of. From the human side, this relationship is accomplished through prayers, offerings, and sacrifices made at the various shrines and altars of the gods. The gods themselves tend to fall into the typical Animistic categories: inanimate objects (rocks, trees, etc.), heavenly objects (sun, stars, etc.), animals and ancestor spirits.

Essential Beliefs
God
Most animistic tribal groups believe in an all-powerful, all-knowing God who was responsible for creating the world and all in it. They also generally acknowledge numerous lesser supernatural spirits which interact with the material world from their position in the spirit world.

Man
Mankind is generally understood to be one part of the "circle of life" which has responsibilities for helping maintain the balance between the material and spiritual parts of reality. It is up to human beings to live harmoniously in the world in relationship with all other living things and with the gods.

Salvation
The concept of salvation, in tribal religions, deals primarily with the obligation to take care of human responsibilities which relate to maintaining harmony in the universe. There are things humans must do to fulfill their obligations to the gods. When this is done well, the gods also make life go well for the humans. This includes helping human beings navigate this life and move smoothly into the next.

Explanation of the Major Far Eastern Thought Groups

Hinduism
Buddhism
Hare Krishna
Sikhism

Hinduism

Background
The word Hindu is derived from *Sindhu,* the Sanskrit word for the inhabitants of India's Indus River region. The English term Hinduism was introduced in the 19th century referring to India's religious, philosophical, and cultural tradition. Most of the 800 million Hindus are found in India, claiming 90% of its population. Others live in Nepal, Mauritius, Fiji, Guyana, Suriname, Bangladesh, Malaysia, Trinidad and Tobago, and Bhutan.

Hinduism originated among Aryan peoples in the Indus Valley about 1500 B.C. They conquered the Indian subcontinent bringing with them their religion. As the Aryans conquered India, much of the invaded group's religions were also absorbed.

The earliest stage of Hinduism was the Animistic pre-Vedic period. The Vedic period began around 1500 B.C. when the Aryans taught their Sanskrit scriptures, called the Vedas, to the native population. This turned the population from Animism to Far Eastern Thought.

The Upanishad period began around 600 B.C. The Upanishads are teachings based on the Vedas, but more philosophical. Vedic religion synthesized the gods into a single pantheistic principle (the absolute universal soul, impersonal life force, cosmos, or Brahman).

Hinduism has six philosophical schools. They include: 1) *samkhya* - an atheistic and dualistic school, 2) yoga - adds worship of God and physical discipline to *samkhya,* 3) *nyaya* - a rationalistic form of thought, 4) *vaisheshika* - classifies all of reality into certain categories, 5) *vedanta* - stresses the identity between god and the soul (Brahman-atman), and 6) *mimamsa* interprets the Vedas literally.

Basic Beliefs and Practices
1. Brahman - The concept of the eternal *Trimutri,* or Three-in-One God. This emphasizes impersonal manifestations of the oneness of *Brahman* consisting of *Brahma* - the Creator; *Vishnu* - the Preserver; and *Shiva* - the Destroyer.
2. Submission to Fate - Man is part of *Brahman* (the universal absolute) which determines how each person lives.

3. The Caste System - Individuals are born into a particular caste (social class) based on the law of karma. Each must remain in that station of life. Change is possible only in the next life.

The major categories are *Brahmins* (priests), *Kshatriyas* (warriors and rulers), *Vaishyas* (merchants), and *Shudras* (workers). The three higher castes fully participate in society. The *Shudras* are unclean outcastes, or untouchables.

4. The Law of Karma - A person's every action has consequences. Good actions create good karma and bad actions create bad karma which is carried over from one lifetime to the next. A person's present life was determined in previous lifetimes. The goal is to accumulate enough good karma to end the birth, death and rebirth cycle and merge with the impersonal life force.

5. Reincarnation - The chain of rebirths in which pieces of the life force move to higher or lower states through successive lives. All life progresses from lower forms up through human life, the highest level. One then ascends from the lower castes to the highest caste of the Brahmins where the individual may shed material existence and merge with the impersonal body of life force.

6. Moksha - The final stage when the life force is liberated from the chain of rebirths and is united with the "cosmos."

7. Yoga - Physical disciplines that control the body and emotions to help accumulate good karma.

8. Dharma - Each person's duty (the "Law of Moral Order"), based on their caste and stage of life, necessary to attain moksha.

Essential Beliefs
God

Ultimate reality is an impersonal and philosophical absolute which is the ultimate manifestation of oneness (the impersonal life force). Hindus worship thousands of gods which are all manifestations of Brahman.

Man

Humans are manifestations of the impersonal life force (*Brahman*) at the upper levels of the reincarnation process. Their personal nature is an illusion so they are ultimately without individual self or self-worth.

Salvation

Escape from the recurring cycles of life and absorption into the impersonal life force (*Brahman*) is the ultimate goal of Hinduism. There are three "ways" to achieve this:
1. The way of knowledge - Giving of one's life to Brahman by mystical identification (a philosophical approach).
2. The way of devotion - Commitment to worship of a particular god who will resolve the karma problem (a worship approach).
3. The way of works - The observance of all Hindu laws and obligations (a works approach).

Buddhism

Background

Buddhism's founder was Siddhartha Gautama ("the Buddha" - ca. 560 - 480 BC), a Hindu prince. Gautama lived in luxury and was protected from the world's misery. One day he ventured beyond his compound and, for the first time, saw and realized suffering existed. At age 29, he renounced his wealth and began a quest for life's meaning.

Gautama submitted to different Hindu masters but was unsatisfied, and for six years practiced extreme self-denial. Finally, he discovered the principle of the "Middle Path," keeping himself from the extremes of either self-denial or self-gratification. Eventually, while in deep meditation, he achieved a state of "enlightenment" and gained the title of the "Buddha" (Enlightened One).

Gautama proclaimed his message throughout northern India for 45 years. After his death, the religion spread incorporating divergent beliefs into his teachings. Eventually Buddhism split into two major groups, *Theravada* or *Hinayana* (The Lesser Vehicle) and *Mahayana* (The Greater Vehicle).

Theravada Buddhism:
- Conservative tendencies
- Emphasis on Buddhist scriptures
- Concern for wisdom
- Salvation is reached by self-effort
- Monasticism and priests
- Atheism

Mahayana Buddhism:
- Liberal tendencies
- Emphasis on meditation
- Salvation by faith in Gautama
- Encourages laymen to practice the faith
- Polytheism and idolatry

Buddhism claims it evolved into different forms to be relevant to every culture and generation. Consequently, little "pure"

Buddhism is now practiced. What is seen is a mixture of Taoism, Confucianism, and ancestor worship. An estimated 300 - 500 million people worldwide are Buddhists. The religion is dominant in China, Japan, Korea, and Southeast Asia.

Basic Beliefs and Practices
The Four Noble Truths
1. Life is full of pain and suffering.
2. Suffering is caused by desire.
3. Desire is eliminated by following the eightfold path.

The Eightfold Path
The Eightfold Path is a guide to enlightenment which leads to *Nirvana* (see definition below). The Eightfold Path can be divided into three categories.

Issues of Wisdom
1. Right knowledge - Understanding things as they really are.
2. Right aspirations (intentions) - Commitment to self-improvement.

Issues of Ethical Conduct
3. Right speech - Abstain from false speech.
4. Right conduct - Abstain from harming others, theft, and sexual misconduct.
5. Right livelihood - Not dealing in weapons, living beings, meat production or intoxicants.

Issues of Mental Development
6. Right effort - Maintain wholesome states (thoughts, words and deeds) and avoid unwholesome ones.
7. Right mindfulness (self-analysis) - Contemplate the body, feelings, and states of mind.
8. Right Concentration - Contemplate wholesome thoughts and actions.

Since Buddhism emerged out of Hinduism, they have several common beliefs.

- *Nirvana* - Sanskrit for "extinction" or "blowing out." The ultimate goal of Buddhist spiritual practice is the end of the cycle of births and rebirths. The person ceases to exist as an individual and the life force merges with the impersonal cosmos ending all desire and suffering.
- *Karma* - Happiness and suffering in this life results from deeds in past lives, or actions in the present one, which either generate or eliminate suffering. "Bad" karma produces suffering while "good" karma prevents suffering. The individual has free will but carries the baggage of previous lives.
- **Reincarnation** - Every living creature (including animals) has a soul (life force) which reincarnates in a new physical expression when an old one ends. This cycle of rebirths continues until an individual reaches enlightenment which catapults him or her into *Nirvan*a where suffering ceases.

Essential Beliefs
God
1. *Theravada* Buddhism - No personal God exists, only an impersonal cosmos encompassing all reality.
2. *Mahayana* Buddhism - Many gods exist, one of which is Gautama. This form combines Buddhist beliefs with Taoism, Confucianism, or other religious systems. The structure of reality is still understood as the impersonal cosmos with which humanity is seeking to merge.

Man
Human beings are a manifestation of the impersonal cosmos stuck in endless cycles of rebirth without individual self or self-worth.

Salvation
Salvation is reaching *Nirvana*. The key is to achieve enlightenment and eliminate desire by gaining wisdom (*Theravada*) or placing one's faith in Gautama, meditating, and repeating the names of *Bodhisattvas* - advanced devotees who postpone *Nirvana* to assist others (*Mahayana*).

Hare Krishna

Background

Hare Krishna began in the 15th century A.D. when Chaitanya Mahaprabu (regarded as an incarnation of Krishna) developed it from Vishnu Hinduism. Hinduism regards Krishna as the 8th incarnation of Vishnu (the Preserver and one of the Hindu trinity of deities). Chaitanya however, regarded Krishna as the supreme Lord in order to make philosophical Hinduism more appealing by personalizing God. In this religion, people gain a personal relationship with Krishna by chanting his names as a mantra: "Hare Krishna, Hare Krishna, Krishna, Krishna, Hare, Hare, Hare Rama, Hare Rama, Rama, Rama, Hare, Hare." The word *Krishna* means "the all-attractive." *Hare* is "the energy of God." *Rama* means "the greatest pleasure."

Hare Krishna came to America in 1965 when Swami A. C. Bhaktivedanta Prabhupada (1896 - 1977) founded the International Society for Krishna Consciousness (ISKCON). Prabhupada's writings, English translations and commentaries of Hindu scriptures, included the *Bhagavad Gita*, the *Bhagavata Purana*, and the *Caitanya Caritamrita*. Before his death, he commissioned eleven commissioners to succeed him. Hare Krishna today has an estimated 3,000 core members and about 250,000 lay constituents worldwide.

ISKCON is run by two boards – one focuses on spiritual practices and the other on administration. It is organized into two sectors. Sector one is an order of monks and priests who live at a temple. The other sector consists of members living in general society.

Male monks shave their heads, except for a patch called a *sikha*, receive a Sanskrit name, and wear robes. Single monks wear saffron robes, while married ones wear white. Females wear Indian saris and do not shave their heads. Outside members wear regular clothing, follow vegetarian diets, pray and chant at home, and go to temple for "Sunday Feast."

Basic Beliefs and Practices

Hare Krishna doctrine has much in common with conventional Hinduism. Their sacred text is the *Bhagavad Gita* which contains conversations between Lord Krishna and a soldier named Arjuna.

A number of distinctive beliefs, however, depart from traditional Hindu doctrine.

- The primary goal of life is to break from repetitive reincarnations and return to God. Body and soul are not the same and death is a transition to the next phase of life. An individual's acts determine if karmic movement is up, down, or out of the reincarnation cycle. Breaking away is attained by chanting the mantra, putting one in harmony with Krishna.
- Krishna is the Supreme God with whom individuals achieve a personal relationship. Jesus is understood to be a representative of Krishna.
- Hell is temporary for people who have sinned greatly while on earth. Heaven is also temporary for people who have progressed in their quest for eternity but have not achieved the full qualifications for ending the cycles of reincarnation.
- Eating food offered to Krishna is an act of communion which purifies the body. Krishna devotees reject sinful living which includes eating meat, using drugs and alcohol, illicit sex, and gambling.
- Devotees practice the "Nine Processes of Devotional Service." These are:
  1. Hearing about God.
  2. Chanting God's names.
  3. Reading and associating with devotees.
  4. Serving in the temple.
  5. Worshiping by preparing food and decorating his idol.
  6. Praying.
  7. Encouraging others to chant.
  8. Developing an intimate relationship with God.
  9. Giving everything one has to God.

Essential Beliefs
God

There is one God, Krishna, who is the eternal, all-knowing, omnipresent, and all-powerful, personality of Godhead who created all. He is the seed-giving father to all living beings and the energy of the eternal cosmic creation. Other incarnations of Godhead are expansions, or parts, of Krishna. Krishna expresses himself both personally and impersonally.

Man
Humans were originally servants of God in the spiritual world. Some turned away from him because of a desire to experience his position. Those rebels were sent to this material world to work through reincarnations in order to progress back to the spiritual world.

Salvation
Salvation is liberation from the bonds of material reality. It is earned by chanting, hearing and singing, meditating, and worshiping. One's deeds in all reincarnated lives are judged positively or negatively based on karma. When good deeds have atoned for bad, a person can realize oneness with Krishna, cease the cycles of rebirth, and return to the eternal spiritual world.

Sikhism

Background

Sikhism was founded by Guru Nanak (1469 - 1539) in the 15th century A.D. in the Punjab area of India. It was a combination of Hinduism and Islam. Nanak taught devotion, brotherhood, charity, obedience, patience, humility, and piety. One of his most essential sayings was "Realization of Truth is higher than all else. Higher still is truthful living." Followers are called Sikhs, meaning disciples. Throughout the centuries Sikhs have endured wars and conflicts with both Hindus and Muslims in India.

Nanak was followed by nine other gurus until 1708. Its holy book is called the *Adi Granth* written by various gurus between 1469 and 1708. The other gurus included Guru Amar Das (1479 - 1574), Guru Angad Dev (1504 - 1552), Guru Har Krishan (1556 - 1564), Guru Ram Das (1534 - 1581), Guru Arjan Dev (1563 - 1606), Guru Hargobind (1599 - 1644), Guru Har Rai (1630 - 1661), Guru Tegh Bahadur (1621 - 1675), and Guru Gobind Singh (1666 - 1708).

Sikhs came to North America in 1897 when Sikh British soldiers from India served in western Canada. In 1908, several thousand Sikhs from India immigrated to California. In 1969, they built the largest Sikh temple in the world in Yuba City, California. The chief American Sikh organization is the Sikh Council of North America. About 500,000 Sikhs are estimated to live in North America.

Basic Beliefs and Practices

Sikh practices revolve around several key principles established by Guru Nanak and his successors. They include the following:

- *Māyā* is the illusion or "unreality" of the values of the world including ego, anger, greed, attachment, and lust – known as the Five Evils.
- *Nśabad* (the divine Word) is the totality of the divine revelation. Gurus (teachers) are the voice of God for knowledge and salvation.
- *Nām* is repetition of the name of God with inward, personal devotion.
- *Kirat karō* is a balance of work, worship, and charity, and defending the rights of all people.
- *Cha dī kalā*, is an optimistic view of life.

- *Va chakkō* is the concept of sharing of material needs.
- Sikhs assert that all people of all races are equal in God's eyes. Men and women are equal and share the same rights, and women are even allowed to lead in prayers.

Sikhs have a number strict prohibitions:
1. *Cutting hair*: Sikhs are forbidden to cut their beards or hair.
2. *Intoxication*: Consumption of alcohol, drugs, tobacco, and other intoxicants is not allowed.
3. *Adultery*: Spouses must be physically and mentally faithful to one another.
4. *Blind spirituality*: Superstitions and rituals should not be observed or followed, including pilgrimages, fasting, ritual purification, or circumcision.
5. *Material obsession*: Obsession with material wealth is not encouraged.
6. *Sacrifice of creatures*: The practice of widows throwing themselves on the funeral fires of their husbands, ritual animal sacrifice, etc. are forbidden.
7. *Non-family-oriented living*: A Sikh is encouraged NOT to live as a recluse, beggar, yogi, monastic (monk/nun) or celibate. Sikhs are to live as saint-soldiers.
8. *Worthless talk*: Bragging, lying, slander, "back-stabbing," etc. are not permitted.
9. *Priestly class*: Sikhism does not have priests.
10. *Eating*: Eating meat killed in a ritualistic manner is not allowed.
11. *Sexual relations*: Premarital or extramarital sexual relations are not permitted.

Essential Beliefs
God

As is taught in Islam, Sikhs believe God is one and is the eternal, sovereign, all-powerful, all-knowing, Creator. At the same time, the Hindu concepts of karma and reincarnation are taught.

God both transcends and indwells the universe. He is the abstract principle of truth and has never known an incarnation. Neither can He be defined. However, God is personal in that He can be loved and honored. Nanak, the first guru, called God the "true name" (Sat

Nam) because he wanted to avoid any term implying God could be limited. The Christian doctrine of the Trinity is rejected.

Man

Humans are separated from God because of self-centeredness and willful ignorance. Consequently, people are bound up in the process known as transmigration of the soul – continual birth, death, and rebirth (reincarnation). The next life is dependent on the law of karma, a notion that one's thoughts, words, and deeds have a direct impact on future reincarnations. The goal of Sikhism is to break this cycle.

Salvation

The endless cycles of reincarnation are caused by selfish desire and ignorance of God. It is believed that these cycles may be ended by full devotion to God. Life's ultimate goals are liberation from continual birth and rebirth, and union with God. Salvation is achieved by obedience to the above principles and devotion to God who reveals himself and allows humans to meditate on His name and nature.

Explanation of the Major non-Christian Theistic Groups

Islam
Judaism
Cultural Christianity
Jehovah's Witnesses
Mormonism
Baha'i

Islam

Background

Islam means "submission." A Muslim is "one who submits" to the will of God (Allah). Islam has a strict unitarian understanding of God that combines elements of Judaism and Christianity. Its founder, Mohammed, is considered the last and greatest of the prophets.

Mohammed was born in Mecca in 570 A.D., in Arabia. His father died before his birth and his mother died when he was six. His grandfather kept him for a short time, but he was raised primarily by his uncle. He did a lot of traveling with his uncle and encountered people of different religions who influenced his thinking.

When he was 25 years old, Mohammed married a wealthy widow fifteen years his elder. None of their children survived except a daughter.

In that era, Arabians were polytheistic and "Allah" was one of their gods. Mohammed, disturbed by this idolatry, concluded that Allah was the only true God. Starting in 610 A.D., Mohammed supposedly received revelations from the angel Gabriel. After his death in 632 A.D., his followers collected his revelations in the Koran.

At first, Mohammed and his few followers were persecuted. On July 16, 622 A.D., he escaped assassination and fled to the city of Yathrib (Medina). This escape, called the *Hegira* (flight), marked the official beginning of Islam.

Mohammed established a theocracy in Medina combining politics with his new religion. He replenished Medina's treasury by plundering caravans going to Mecca. This led to a war in which Mohammed prevailed. Most Arab tribes, along with those in Mecca, were forced to adopt Islam. After Mohammed's death, his successors conquered Syria, Jerusalem, Egypt, Persia, and Mesopotamia. War was the primary way Islam spread.

Main Islamic Groups

Islam consists of several denominations with similar beliefs but with some differences. The largest denominations are the Sunni and the Shia. 85% of the world's Muslims are Sunni and 14% are Shia. The other 1% consists of small sects. This division has caused numerous wars.

Sunni

The Sunnah (the record of Mohammed in the Koran), and the hadith (explanations attributed to Mohammad) are the foundations of Sunni doctrine. Four caliphs were Mohammad's rightful successors to rule the Muslim world. Controversy over the fourth caliph split Islam into the two branches. Sunnis argued that later caliphs had to be elected.

Shia

The Shia, conversely, said Islam's leaders (Imams) must descend from the fourth caliph, Mohammed's cousin and son-in law, Ali Talib. Imams rule by divine appointment with absolute authority on matters of theology.

Basic Beliefs and Practice
The Five Doctrines:
1. Allah is the one true God.
2. Allah has sent many prophets to guide men. The Koran mentions 28 (most from the Old and New Testaments). Jesus was a sinless prophet, but Mohammed was the last and greatest.
3. The Koran is the greatest of four inspired books including the *Tauret* (the Pentateuch), the *Zabur* (Psalms), and the *Injil* (Evangel of Jesus).
4. Angels are Allah's intermediaries to man. Fallen angels are demons.
5. At the Day of Judgment, everyone's deeds will be weighed to determine their eternal destiny in Heaven or Hell.

The Five Pillars:
1. Recitation of Islam's creed (the *Shahadah*). - "There is no God but Allah, and Mohammed is his prophet."
2. Prayer five times a day facing Mecca (*Salat*).
3. Almsgiving *(Zakat)*.
4. Fasting during daylight hours in the month of Ramadan (*Sawm*).
5. The pilgrimage to Mecca at least once in a lifetime, if able (*Hajj*).

Essential Beliefs
God
Allah is the only God. He is totally transcendent and human beings cannot know him personally – they can only know about him by his revelation. The Trinity is rejected as polytheism. Believing Jesus is the Son of God is blasphemy. Islam teaches a rigid doctrine of predestination and says evil and good come from Allah. Whatever Allah chooses is right in all situations.

Man
Human beings are special creations of God and are not sinful by nature, only by act. They have no need to be saved from sin, only to act correctly.

Salvation
Correct actions are defined by the Koran. God keeps track of a person's right and wrong acts. At death, the good and bad deeds are weighed. Those with greater good than bad may enter Heaven. Even so, there is no guarantee of salvation. It is only as "Allah wills."

Judaism

Background

The story of the Jewish faith begins when God chose Abraham to form the basis of a special people who would represent him to the rest of the world. Abraham's descendants eventually conquered what became the land of Israel and set up a kingdom. This kingdom ultimately divided into two kingdoms, Judah and Israel, which were both later conquered and the people disbursed and taken into exile.

In due time the Jewish people returned to Israel, but were successively ruled from the outside by Babylon, Persia, Greece, and Rome. After a rebellion against the Romans, the country was destroyed and the people disbursed throughout the world. They did not have their own nation again until 1948.

Over the centuries, the Jews have somehow maintained their identity, even though they have been repeatedly dispersed throughout the world.

There are four primary Jewish groups.

1. Orthodox - This group observes most of the traditional dietary and ceremonial laws. They also affirm the inspiration of the Old Testament with the Torah being most important.
2. Reformed - The Reformed branch is the home of liberal Judaism where Talmudic practices and precepts have been put aside for an ethical system based on a monotheistic philosophy.
3. Conservative - Between the Orthodox and Reform groups lie the Conservatives. This group retains the feasts and many traditional customs, but reinterprets the Law to make it relevant to modern thought and culture.
4. Hasidic - The Hasidic Jews are the ultra-orthodox and mystical group.

Basic Beliefs and Practices

While there is a lot of variety within the Jewish community, there are two elements which establish their identity as a people.

1. Worship - Ritual and ceremony are important to consecrate life with God in a calendar of daily, weekly, and yearly celebrations. The best known festivals include Passover, the Festival of Weeks, the Feast of Tabernacles, Yom Kippur (Day of Atonement), and Rosh Hashanah (Jewish New Year). The

purpose of the celebrations is to remember their sacred history. Stories, both Biblical and non-Biblical, relating God's deliverance are told over and over.

Since the destruction of the temple in Jerusalem, Jews have gathered for worship in the synagogue. Ritual, prayer and the study of the Law serve as the replacement for the sacrifices once held in the temple.

2. Morality - Judaism has a strong emphasis on morality and ethics. The traditional idea behind the Jewish ethic is that God ordains a certain way to live which has been passed down through the generations.

This ethical emphasis is primarily based on the teachings of the Torah (first five books of the Old Testament). Sin is understood to be specific acts, so Jews have developed rules of behavior and codes of conduct. From time to time, movements have emerged to get back to the original meaning of Torah. But because of their understanding of sin, this legalistic approach is difficult to replace.

Morality is heavily tilted toward the good of the community and contains a strong sense of social and economic justice.

Essential Beliefs
God

Judaism is solidly monotheistic. God is viewed as a complete unity, powerful, just, merciful and loving. He is a personal being who has a relationship with mankind. He continually works in the world and offers humans the opportunity to fulfill their obligations to him. The Holy Spirit is recognized simply to be the expression of God's interaction with humanity in this world.

Man

Mankind is viewed as a special creation of God who was created in his image. Man has a great responsibility to live rightly before God. In Jewish theology, the distinguishing mark of humans is their ability to make ethical choices. Man also has a responsibility to help order the world in accordance with God's purposes.

Salvation

Sin, in Jewish theology, is not a state, it is simply an act. This is the reason the law is so important. The foundational belief is that if individuals simply obey the Jewish law, they avoid sin. When they fail, they only need to come to God in repentance.

There is, therefore, no need for a Savior. Forgiveness for sin is accomplished by sacrifices, penitence, good deeds and a little of God's grace. External things like Sabbath observance, food preparation, dietary rules and holy days are the means by which people are able to please God.

Cultural Christianity

Background

Up until the last two to three generations, the primary worldview foundation in America was Theism – primarily, Christian Theism. This has been described in various ways. Sometimes America has simply been called a "Christian nation" or it is not uncommon to hear a reference to the "Judeo-Christian ethic." The point is that the nation was founded by Christians who built its foundational institutions on Christian ideas. Of course, America is a prime example of a country that is considered Christian, but is certainly not the only one which fits into this category. A great deal of Europe can also be said to fit this mold.

One of the very important principles of biblical Christianity is that every individual must come to Christ based on a personal decision to do so. A person is not a Christian by virtue of having been born in a country or a family with a Christian heritage, nor by having been baptized and raised in a Christian church.

In spite of the true nature of the Christian faith, there are masses of people who define Christianity based on their national or family origin or their affiliation with a Christian church. These people generally know the rituals and church forms and simply self-identify as Christians because they do not follow some other religion.

Basic Beliefs and Practices

One of the things that makes cultural Christianity so difficult to deal with is that from the outside it may look like the real thing. Typically, cultural Christians self-identify as Christians, are a member of some Christian church, and have usually been baptized at some point in their lives.

Participation in the Christian faith by cultural Christians can be quite varied. This variation is expressed in several ways.

Some cultural Christians have not set foot in a church in years. These are people who believe the only requirement for being a Christian is saying they are one. Participation in church or other aspects of the Christian faith are not believed to be necessary to their identity as a Christian.

Others participate on occasion – for instance at Easter and Christmas. These people, also, generally believe they are Christians based purely on self-identification, but also feel a need to occasionally participate in something. Still others are very active in their churches, and may even become church leaders. Many of them believe that their participation in church activities proves that they are Christians. This kind of situation is not at all uncommon in churches which call themselves Christian, but which have a theological position which doesn't require a person to enter into a personal relationship with God through Jesus Christ as the means of their salvation.

The thing that identifies cultural Christians is internal – the fact that they have never repented of sin and invited Christ into their lives. This sometimes makes cultural Christians hard to identify and even harder to witness to. They generally hold to a Christian worldview (which has been hybridized by various non-Christian beliefs), identify with some recognized Christian church, and agree with a Christian understanding of morality (even if they don't completely follow it).

Essential Beliefs
God
Cultural Christians generally, though not always, hold a Theistic worldview and believe in the God of the Bible as the Creator. That being said, there are almost always beliefs from other worldviews which have been allowed to creep in. Some of the more common aberrations may include a belief in the Theory of Evolution or a belief that God is willing to overlook a non-biblical lifestyle. It is also not at all unusual for these people to generally believe in the God of the Bible, yet still make up their own concepts of God because they have no idea what the Bible actually teaches.

Man
Cultural Christians generally hold a view of mankind that is in line with the culture at large. This frequently includes the notion that human beings are basically good and that they are capable of living a life good enough to please God.

Salvation

Cultural Christians generally believe they are going to heaven because they self-identify with the Christian faith. They tend to have no concept of the biblical requirements for salvation or they misunderstand what the Bible teaches about the subject.

Jehovah's Witnesses

Background

In 1870, Charles Taze Russell (1852 - 1916) began an independent Bible study focusing on the second coming of Christ and biblical chronology. In 1879, he founded the monthly publication Zion's *Watch Tower and Herald of Christ's Presence,* which was used by the study groups he established.

Zion's Watchtower and Tract Society was incorporated in 1884 with Russell as president. From 1886 until his death in 1916, Russell wrote a series of books called *Studies in the Scriptures.* Their contents formed the basis of Jehovah's Witnesses' unchristian theology.

Russell was succeeded as president in 1917 by his legal assistant, Joseph Franklin Rutherford. Rutherford continued Russell's authoritarian leadership style. He was imprisoned briefly in 1918 for preaching against military service. He was a charismatic speaker who often railed against Christian churches and biblical scholars. He died in 1942.

Other Jehovah's Witnesses presidents included Nathan H. Knorr (1942 - 1977), Fredrick W. Franz (1977 - 1992), and Milton G. Henschel (1992 - 2000). The organization expanded worldwide under these men's leadership, from about 113,000 in 1942 to more than 6 million in 2000. The current president is Don Adams.

Beliefs and Practices

There are several distinctive beliefs that characterize the theology and practice of Jehovah's Witnesses.

- The official name of the Jehovah's Witnesses organization is the Watchtower Bible and Tract Society (WBTS).
- The WBTS is regarded as Jehovah God's sole channel for the flow of Biblical truth to men on earth.

- Members attend local congregations called Kingdom Halls and regularly do door-to-door visitation and distribute WBTS literature.
- Jehovah's Witnesses claim the Bible is their only authority. Their official version is *The New World Translation of the Holy Scriptures* (NWT). They claim it is the best translation ever made, but most Greek and Hebrew scholars agree that it is poorly done and extremely biased against the deity of Christ.
- Jehovah's Witnesses deny the Trinity, the divinity of Christ, his bodily resurrection, salvation by grace through faith and eternal punishment of the wicked.
- There is no hell as a place of everlasting punishment for the wicked in Jehovah's Witness theology. They claim that it is: 1) wholly unscriptural; 2) unreasonable; 3) contrary to God's love; and 4) repugnant to justice.
- Over the years, Jehovah's Witnesses have made many prophesies concerning the end of the world which did not come true. Those prophesies were later reinterpreted to make them appear to have come true.

Essential Beliefs
God

The true God's name is Jehovah. His principal attributes are love, wisdom, justice, and power. God is a "spirit being," invisible and eternal, but has a spiritual body and is not omnipresent. The historic Christian doctrine of the Trinity is denied.

In his pre-human existence, Jesus was called "God's only-begotten Son" because Jehovah created him directly. As the "first-born of all creation," Jesus was used by God to create all other things. Jesus became the Messiah at his baptism, was executed on a torture stake, and rose again spiritually. The personality and deity of the Holy Spirit is denied.

Man

God created man in His own image, but Adam and Eve willfully disobeyed God. Thus, humanity lost immortality and must experience physical death. There is no conscious existence at death. The dead go to the common grave of mankind where they are not conscious of anything awaiting the final resurrection.

Salvation

Due to Adam's sin, atonement was required to restore what was lost. Only a perfect human, Jesus Christ, could offer up the equivalent of what Adam lost. He was nailed to a wooden pole and hung there upright. He slept in death for parts of three days. Following that, Jehovah God resurrected him to life as a mighty spirit being.

Requirements for salvation, in addition to faith, include baptism by immersion, active association with the WBTS, righteous conduct, and absolute loyalty to Jehovah. There is no assurance of salvation, only hope for a resurrection. Those who fail to live up to the requirements, or who are disfellowshipped by the WBTS, have no hope of salvation.

Only 144,000 faithful elect Jehovah's Witnesses, known as the "Anointed Class," will go to heaven to rule with Jesus. Most Jehovah's Witnesses hope to be among the "other sheep" or "great crowd" who will be resurrected and live forever in Paradise on earth.

Mormonism

Background

Joseph Smith, Jr. was born December 23, 1805 in Vermont and grew up in Palmyra, New York. According to his own story, in the fall of 1820, as a teenager, Smith wanted to know which church to join. One day he went in the woods near his home to pray about the question. While he was praying, he claimed that God the Heavenly Father and his Son, Jesus, appeared to him. Jesus told him to join none of the churches because they were all in error and corrupt. Jesus told him that in time he would use Smith to restore his true church to the world.

In September of 1823, Joseph said he had a second vision, this time of an angel named Moroni. Moroni showed him a set of golden plates buried near his home that were supposedly a record of ancient Jewish peoples who lived in America. In 1829, Smith translated the plates, and in 1830 published them as *The Book of Mormon*.

Under God's direction, on April 6 1830, Smith and five other men established the restored "Church of Christ" in Fayette, NY. Later, the church's name was changed to the current Church of Jesus Christ of Latter-day Saints (LDS). Because of opposition in New York in 1831, the church migrated to Kirtland, Ohio and later to Independence, Missouri, where they also faced conflict due to rumors that the Mormons (as they came to be known) were practicing polygamy.

So, in 1840, the Mormons moved on to Nauvoo, Illinois. There, in 1844, Smith was arrested, and on June 27, 1844, was assassinated by a mob in Carthage, Ill. Beginning in 1846, Smith's successor, Brigham Young, led the Mormons westward where they settled in what is now Utah.

Basic Beliefs and Practices

The LDS has the following requirements for all faithful members:
1. Faith and Repentance toward the Mormon God (called Heavenly Father).
2. Baptism by immersion in the LDS Church and the laying on of hands to receive the Holy Ghost.
3. Ordination as Aaronic Priests and Melchizedek Priests for all worthy men.

4. Young men are expected to serve a two-year mission for the church.
5. Receiving endowments. These are secret ceremonies in LDS temples necessary to prepare them for life after death.
6. Celestial (Temple) Marriage for time and eternity.
7. Participating in baptisms and ordinances for the salvation of the dead.
8. Observing the "Word of Wisdom." This means abstaining from all alcohol, tobacco, and caffeine products.
9. Tithing 10% of one's income and attending weekly Sacrament Meetings.
10. Following the teachings of The Four Standard Works (*the King James Bible, The Book of Mormon, Doctrine and Covenants,* and *The Pearl of great Price*), as well as those of the Living Prophet (the LDS President).

Essential Beliefs
God

God was once a man, as we now are, who was exalted by his god to godhood (exaltation) after living a faithful Mormon life on his planet. In his exalted life, he lives with his wife (or wives), and the two of them produce spirit children. In addition to our God, there are also countless other gods in the universe. God did not create the world from nothing ("ex nihilo"), but organized earth out of pre-existent matter.

Jesus (Jehovah) was the first born spirit son of the heavenly parents who later attained godhood. He was later sent to earth as the "only-begotten" Son of God in the flesh. The Holy Ghost is another god but does not have a body of flesh and bones.

Man

God and his wife procreate spirit children in a preexistent world who are later born on earth in physical bodies. Physical birth is the first necessary step in the Mormon plan of salvation for the heavenly Father's children to attain exaltation. *All* people, however, are mortal because of the fall of Adam. Thus, Jesus suffered, died, and was raised from the dead to restore immortality to everyone regardless of their faith.

Salvation

All people will be raised to immortality because of Jesus' redemption. After judgment, however, everyone will be sent to one of three levels of heavenly glory based on their works while living on earth. The Celestial Kingdom is the destination for worthy Mormons. All other honorable people will spend eternity in the Terrestrial Kingdom. The Telestial Kingdom will be the home of the ungodly, wicked, and filthy. Only faithful Mormons, who follow all the above requirements will go to the Celestial Kingdom where they may be exalted to godhood.

Worldview Resources

Baha'i Faith

Background

Baha'i originated in Iran in the 19th century. Some Muslims had been waiting for Allah to raise up a new prophet. In 1844, Mirza Ali Mohammed (1819 - 1850) took upon himself the title "The Bab" (the Gate) and proclaimed the soon coming of this prophet. Large numbers of people followed him and became known as Babists. The Persian (Iranian) government and the Islamic clergy partnered together to kill Mirza Ali when he was thirty years of age, declaring him an apostate from Islam. They also massacred more than twenty thousand of his followers.

In 1863, another Persian, named Baha'u'llah (1817 - 1892), claimed to be the prophet that Mirza Ali had predicted. Many followers of the Bab became disciples of the new prophet and changed their name to Baha'i to honor him. Baha'u'llah called upon all people to unite in one common faith to establish abiding peace.

Baha'u'llah was also persecuted. After forty years of imprisonment and exile, he died in 1892 at the age of seventy-five. His son, Abbas Effendi, also known as Abdul-Baha (1844 - 1921), succeeded him. In 1893, the Baha'i religion came to the United States. After Abdul's death in 1921, his grandson, Shoghi Effendi (1897 - 1957), became the new leader.

Effendi died before he was able to appoint a successor. As a result, a new system of leadership was established called the Baha'i Universal House of Justice. It consists of a nine-person board that interprets and applies the laws of Baha'u'llah.

Basic Beliefs and Practices

Baha'is believe in one God who at various times in history sends messengers, which they refer to as "manifestations of God." Through these messengers, God restates his purpose and will in every age. These manifestations provided revelations from God. Abraham, Moses, Krishna, Buddha, Zoroaster, Christ, and Muhammad were manifestations for their times. The current generation's manifestation is Baha'u'llah to whom followers of all religions should now turn for spiritual guidance.

Baha'i's ten basic principles are:
1. The oneness of mankind.

Bridges: How to Share a Witness across Worldview Barriers

2. Independent investigation of truth.
3. The common foundation of all religions.
4. The harmony of science and religion.
5. Equality of men and women.
6. Elimination of all prejudice.
7. Universal education.
8. A solution to the economic problem.
9. A universal language.
10. Universal peace by a world government.

Today, in order to be considered a Baha'i, one must be a formal member of the mainstream Baha'i religious organization and pledge obedience to the Baha'i administrative order. Baha'is seek universal systems of education, human rights, currency, weights, measures, and language, and are very active in United Nations organizations.

Essential Beliefs
God

Baha'is teach that there is only one expression of God who is absolutely indivisible. In concert with Islam, he is considered to be transcendent to the point of total inaccessibility and could never incarnate as a human. God is creator of all things, but not the cause of all things. Rather, all that exists flows eternally out of him. God is the changeless One who is separated from interactive relationship with his created order.

The way God is known is by divine human manifestations who are pure mirrors of his attributes. There have been nine manifestations in the 500,000 year cycle of human history including Abraham, Krishna, Moses, Zoroaster, Buddha, Christ, Mohammad, the Bab, and Baha'u'llah. Baha'u'llah is the supreme manifestation for the current cycle of human history.

Man

Humanity is a creation of God, and men and women of all races are equal in his sight. People of different races should have equal educational and economic opportunity, access to decent living conditions and equal responsibilities. Man is not inherently evil, but has the capacity for doing evil deeds. Each man decides whether to follow God, thus determining his eternal destiny.

Salvation

Salvation is deliverance from the captivity of people's own lower nature. This captivity breeds private despair and threatens social destruction. Salvation means drawing nearer to God and progressing on the path to deep and satisfying happiness. It is obtained by believing in the manifestation of God in the age in which one lives, and by following his teachings. In our current time, this means following the teachings of Baha'u'llah. Humans can realize their true potential and unite with God because he has sent his manifestations to show them the path to spiritual growth.

Explanation of the Major Hybrid Groups

New Age
Unitarian Universalism
Scientology
Christian Science
Unification Church

The New Age Movement

Background

The history of the New Age Movement is difficult, if not impossible to completely trace. Many various religious and spiritual movements and diverse writers have contributed to what became, in the 1970s and 80's, a multi-faceted and broadly defined spiritual movement. Perhaps its earliest roots go back to the Far Eastern traditions of Hinduism and Buddhism along with pre-Christian European paganism. Many ideas from these sources have been introduced or revived in the West over the past century.

Some major teachers whose ideas influenced New Age thinking included Emanuel Swedenborg (1688 - 1772), a Swedish scientist and mystic, German Franz Mesmer (1734 - 1815) who taught a form of healing using "animal magnetism," and Russian mystics Helena Blavatsky (1831 - 1891 - founder of Theosophy), and George Gurdjieff (1872 - 1949).

Other movements that coalesced to form the New Age movements were 19th century Spiritualism (which taught communication with the dead), the New Thought Movement of Phineas Quimby, and Edgar Cayce, a 20th century mystic called the "Sleeping Prophet."

Today a bevy of New Age teachers, writers, and entrepreneurs promote their latest spiritual discoveries. New Age concepts have quietly intruded into various avenues of society including medicine, business, education, art, and even science. A number of celebrities have attached their names to New Age concepts of one kind or another including Oprah Winfrey and Shirley MacClain. Some of the most popular New Age teachers in recent years include Deepak Chopra, James Redfield, Eckhart Tolle, Barbara Marx Hubbard, Christopher Hills, and Marianne Williamson.

Beliefs and Practices

It is impossible to fully summarize the diverse beliefs and practices of the New Age Movement in any coherent systematic way. Nonetheless, researchers have found several common strains running through many of them including the following:

1. Monism - All reality is one – including God, humankind, the universe, time, and space. All is a unitary whole.

2. Pantheism - Everything is God. All (god) is impersonal energy, force, or consciousness.
3. You Are God - The goal of life is to awaken to the god who sleeps at the root of one's being.
4. The Human Problem - New Agers basically deny the existence of sin. People's problem is that they are unaware of their true divinity.
5. Reincarnation - Many New Agers teach that humans go through many lifetimes which will eventually culminate in oneness with the universe. This also includes the Far Eastern concept of positive and negative Karma.
6. Enlightenment - Human ignorance is overcome through enlightenment which can be realized through various techniques including meditation, yoga, past-life regression, trance channeling, crystals, or other occult practices.

Essential Beliefs
God

In New Age belief, the concept of God is rather nebulous. In fact, there are differing views depending on the particular elements that are incorporated into various expressions. In some cases, the concept of God draws from Far Eastern Thought concepts and uses a pantheistic approach. Here, ultimate reality is some form of spiritual life force. Other approaches to New Age incorporate Animistic ideas. In these, the life energy is usually expressed in nature, with man being a part of the "circle of life."

Man

Again, the view of man in New Age belief depends on the particulars of a given expression. Those which follow a Far Eastern Thought approach will see man as an expression of the impersonal life force. This is often expressed by individuals, themselves, being referred to as gods. There is sometimes even an element which incorporates reincarnation, karma and/or evolution of man to a higher form (Age of Aquarius). Those forms which have more Animistic leanings tend to see man as an element of nature and having the ability to connect, somehow, with the earth.

Salvation

Salvation in New Age belief is, once again, influenced by the particular approach taken to specific expressions of the belief. Far Eastern Thought based approaches tend to look to some kind of movement to a higher level of existence – sometimes in a reincarnated life and sometimes in some kind of afterlife. Animistic expressions tend toward an afterlife with some kind of connection with nature.

Unitarian Universalists

Background

The concept of God as a single unitary being – contrary to Christian Trinitarianism – can be traced to the teachings of Arius (A.D. 256 - 336), a pastor in Alexandria, Egypt. He argued that the Bible does not teach a Trinitarian concept of God and that Jesus made no claims to deity. His Unitarian view was rebuked by the Council of Nicea in AD 325. Unitarianism revived after the Protestant Reformation with Michael Servetus (1511 - 1553) in Spain, and Faustus Socinus (1539 - 1604) in Poland. Later, a Hungarian named Frances David (1510 - 1579) led the first movement to be labeled Unitarian.

The first American Unitarian church was King's Chapel in Boston, Massachusetts. In 1786, the previously Episcopalian congregation embraced the Unitarian view. Soon afterward, Harvard University followed suit.

The American Unitarian Association (AUA) was established in 1825 and was led by William Ellery Channing (1780 - 1842), pastor of Federal Street Congregational Church in Boston. Most Unitarian ministers of that time, despite their rejection of Trinitarianism, still relied on the Bible for their theological formulations.

In the 20th century Unitarianism abandoned all biblical authority. In fact, the movement internally debated the very existence of God. Eventually, it came to be dominated by Naturalism and Humanism. This culminated in 1933 with the publishing of the Humanist Manifesto. Half of its signees were Unitarian ministers.

Universalism also emerged at various times throughout the history of the Christian church. It is the theological doctrine that all souls will ultimately be saved and that there is no such thing as hell. Universalism also denies that there is any such thing as miracles, and reject any reference to them in Scripture.

American Universalism developed from the influence of Pietists and Anabaptists in Europe. The first known Universalist church in America was probably the Freedonia Meeting Hall in Newberry County South Carolina. The first General Society was held in 1778 and annual conventions began in 1785. In 1804, the convention changed its name to "The General Convention of Universalists." From this emerged the Universalist Church of America. In 1866, it was known as the Universalist General Convention. In 1942, they changed the name to the Universalist Church of America.

In 1961, the Unitarian churches merged with the Universalist Church of America to form the Unitarian Universalist Association (UUA). The UUA developed into a society focusing on liberal social, political, environmental, and gender-related issues.

One surprising modern trend is the growth of neo-paganism and witchcraft in some UUA congregations. We have also witnessed a decline in the influence of Secular Humanism with the rise of Postmodernism.

Basic Beliefs and Practices

No specific doctrinal perspective is required for membership in the Unitarian Universalist church and members are not bound by any statement of belief or creed. Most Unitarian Universalists maintain that human reason, intuition, and scientific research are the only reliable sources for discovering all truth. Generally, they reject supernatural sources of knowledge – especially divine sources of revelation such as the Bible or other religious texts. That being said, neo-pagan Unitarian Universalists do accept supernatural beliefs that defy naturalistic presuppositions.

Essential Beliefs
God

No particular belief about God is taught nor is any doctrinal belief stated concerning the existence or nature of a god. It is each individual's choice what, if any, concept of deity they wish to accept. Historically, Unitarians rejected the Christian doctrine of the Trinity as polytheistic. Currently, some Unitarian Universalists profess belief in gods and goddesses of various numbers and kinds.

Unitarian Universalists who believe that Jesus actually lived – and many do not – regard Him as a moral teacher or religious reformer. They reject the claim that He was the unique incarnation of God.

Man

Unitarian Universalists reject the biblical doctrine of original sin. They teach that basically all people are good and have no need for spiritual redemption from the effects of sin.

Salvation

Salvation, in Unitarian Universalist belief, is finding one's own self-fulfillment and truth. There is no essential need for the traditional concepts of Christian redemption and salvation. Since men are not understood to be sinners, they do not need forgiveness from sin.

Those who do believe in some concept of existence after this life describe it in vague terms. Heaven and hell are seen to be only states of mind in this life that may or may not extend beyond death.

Some who follow a neo-pagan approach in the UUA probably have adopted Eastern or New Age concepts of reincarnation or spiritualism. Nearly all Unitarian Universalists reject any concept of an eternal hell for punishment of sin.

Scientology

Background

Scientologists believe L. Ron Hubbard was a modern genius who discovered the answers to life's questions and unraveled the secrets of our past, present, and future existences. His writings and speeches are considered absolutely authoritative, especially his book *Dianetics: The Modern Science of Mental Health*.

Lafayette Ronald Hubbard was born in Nebraska in 1911. He spent most of his childhood on his grandfather's Montana ranch while his parents served overseas in the U.S. Navy. Hubbard later stated that visits with parents to Asia in the 1920s introduced him to Eastern philosophies and religions

As a young man, Hubbard developed a career as a science fiction writer and claimed to have explored the world. He also claimed that he received near fatal wounds in World War II. While recovering, he formulated his novel psychological theories that were revealed in his 1950 book *Dianetics: The Modern Science of Mental Health*.

In 1954, Hubbard incorporated the Church of Scientology in order to promote his ideas using a religious facade. The official name of the church is "Church of Scientology International." His books and church spread worldwide, but Hubbard became a recluse. He spent most of his last years aboard his yacht being waited on hand-and-foot. He died inauspiciously in 1986.

Researchers not associated with the Church of Scientology have documented numerous inaccuracies in Hubbard's account of his life. They allege he fabricated and exaggerated many of his personal claims and plagiarized many ideas he used in his writings.

The name Scientology comes from the Latin *scio*, which means " to know" and the Greek word *logos*, meaning "the word or outward form by which the inward thought is expressed and made known." Thus, Scientology means knowing about knowing.

Beliefs and Practices

Hubbard taught the following key concepts.
- The universe is composed of "the Eight Dynamics." These are eight levels of existence which have "Dynamic" urges to survive.
  1. Self - surviving as an individual.
  2. Creativity - survival of the family unit by bearing children.

3. Group - surviving as a group (a company, state, nation, race or any group).
4. Mankind - survival of all mankind.
5. Life Forms - survival of life forms (animals, birds, insects, fish and vegetation).
6. Physical Universe - survival of the physical universe itself.
7. Spiritual Dynamic - survival as spiritual beings.
8. Infinity - the allness of all.

- The human mind consists of two contents: (1) the Analytical mind (the conscious, rational, and problem solving part of one's mind), and (2) the Reactive mind (the part of the mind not under a person's rational, conscious control or awareness).
- As a person goes through life, he or she accumulates *engrams*. These are unconscious mental images recorded in the reactive mind that have negative effects on a person's life.
- Using a Method developed by L. Ron Hubbard, called Danetics, a person can remove engrams and their negative effects from the mind. The word "Dianetics" comes from the Greek words *dia*, meaning "through" and *nous*, meaning "soul."
- A specially trained Scientology counselor, called an Auditor, conducts intense Dianetic sessions called auditing.
- The Auditor uses an instrument called an E-Meter (Electro-psychometer) in the auditing process. The Preclear (person being audited) holds a metal tube in each hand wired to the E-meter which emits a slight electric current. The auditor watches a gauge to detect engrams as the person answers questions.
- Eventually the Preclear will reach a state of mind called "Clear." "Clear" supposedly eliminates all engrams and their ill effects on the mind and body.

Essential Beliefs
God

The Church of Scientology International has no clear definition of the nature or person of God. References to a Supreme Being are rare in Scientology literature. When there is a reference to it, it is called the "eight dynamic" or "infinity." The Supreme Being is defined in vague, pantheistic terms as embracing the "allness of all."

Man

Human beings are considered to be eternal spirits (Thetans) migrating from one body to another over time. Engrams are stored in one's "reactive mind" and learned from one's past lives, prenatal experience, and early childhood. These engrams prevent individuals from realizing their innate divinity and experiencing a happy and fulfilled life using their analytical minds.

Salvation

Engrams are removed from the mind only by an expensive process of Dianetic counseling. A person who has attained Clear may need further auditing to remove engrams held over from previous lives. Auditing sessions may cost as much as $1,000 per hour.

A person will experience many Thetans (reincarnations) in many lives over thousands of years. Eventually, Thetans can liberate themselves completely from the material world, attain total spiritual awareness and become one with infinity.

Christian Science

Background

Mary Ann Morse Baker (1821 - 1910) was a frail young woman who suffered many illnesses. However, in 1866, she claimed she discovered the secret of "Divine Science" after being healed miraculously from a crippling fall. In 1875, she founded the Christian Science Association in Lynn, Massachusetts and published her book, *Science and Health with Key to the Scriptures* (S&H). She taught her principles of divine healing and her book became a best-seller.

After two earlier failed marriages, Mary married Asa Albert Eddy (d. 1882) in 1877 and together they established "The Church of Christ, Scientist" (Christian Science) with its headquarters in Boston, Massachusetts. Christian Science interprets the Bible in light of Mrs. Eddy's writings, particularly S&H, in which she interprets it according to her metaphysical presuppositions.

Basic Beliefs and Practice

Christian Science does not have an organizational creed, but certain doctrines and practices define its uniqueness.

1. The Bible, regarded as its primary authority, must be interpreted according to the principles related in S&H. Mrs. Eddy ascribed arbitrary spiritual meanings to common biblical terms. For example "Jerusalem" is defined as "Mortal belief and knowledge obtained from the five corporeal senses" (S&H, p. 589). "Holy Ghost" is defined as "Divine Science; the development of eternal Life, Truth, and Love" (S&H, p. 588). Her allegorical Bible reading leaves it open to whatever interpretation she chose.
2. Jesus Christ is the means by which individuals achieve physical healing. Healing also involves character transformation, harmony in relationships, schooling, career, marriage, mental health and every other aspect of life, all accomplished through prayer.
3. For practitioners, physical healing confirms the primary mission of Christian Science – to heal "the sins of the world" through understanding the power of Christ, or divine Truth.

4. Understanding the nature of God and His laws is necessary to heal systematically and consistently. When a person prays with understanding, healing occurs. Jesus' healing work provides the foremost example of how his followers also can turn to God's omnipotent love for healing.
5. An important Christian Science practice is studying the weekly Lesson-Sermon outlined in The Christian Science Quarterly. It includes excerpts from the Bible and S&H. It also contains a sermon read in Sunday services throughout the world.
6. Sunday School is provided for children and teenagers. Wednesday evening meetings include readings from the Bible and S&H on current topics. Member's testimonies of healing through prayer are also commonly shared.

Essential Beliefs
God

God is not considered to be a person but is "incorporeal, divine, supreme, infinite Mind, Spirit, Soul, Principle, Life, Truth, Love" (S&H, p. 465). These synonymous terms refer to one absolute God. They express the nature, essence, and wholeness of Deity. The attributes of God are justice, mercy, wisdom, goodness, and so on (S&H, p. 465).

The Trinity is redefined as life, truth, and love. God's essential essence is spirit or mind and only that which reflects His nature is real. Thus, matter does not really exist. Jesus was a discoverer of the Christ-Ideal but there is an essential difference between Jesus the man and the "Christ Principle" which came upon Him as He comprehended it.

Man

People are "Divine Spirits." Since matter does not exist and humanity reflects God's nature, human beings are not really made of matter. "Spirit is God, and man is His image and likeness. Therefore man is not material; he is spiritual" (S&H, p. 468). Since only those ideas that reflect God's nature are actually real, then sin, death, disease, and pain are not real, but only illusions.

Salvation

Since matter, sin, disease, and death are illusions and unreal, people are not subject to them. Thus when people fully realize this principle, disease should disappear. Since God and man are immortal spirit or mind, death is also only an illusion. It is a transition from the illusion of the material to ultimate reality of immortal spirit. Salvation involves an individual overcoming the false idea that he or she exists based on a realization of our divine spirit and mind. "We acknowledge that the crucifixion of Jesus and his resurrection served to uplift faith to understand eternal life, even the allness of Soul, Spirit, and the nothingness of matter" (S&H, p. 497).

Bridges: How to Share a Witness across Worldview Barriers

The Unification Church of Rev. Sun Myung Moon

Background

On January 6, 1920, Yong Myung Moon was born in northern Korea. Moon claims that at age 16 (1936) he saw Jesus Christ who changed his name to Sun Myung Moon (Sun "Shining" Moon). Moon was imprisoned during the Japanese military occupation of Korea. After World War II, he began preaching a set of unusual new doctrines.

In 1948 North Korean communists arrested Moon. He was liberated in 1950 during the Korean War and went to Seoul. In 1952 he released *The Divine Principle*, a compilation of his doctrines. On May 1, 1954, he established "The Holy Spirit Association for the Unification of World Christianity," or the Unification Church (UC). The official name of the church is the Family Federation for World Peace and Unification and is also known informally as the Moonies.

On April 11, 1960, Moon married Hak Ja Han, in what the UC calls the "Marriage of the Lamb" which, they assert, established the "The True Family." During the 1960s, the movement gained converts in Korea.

Moon toured the United States in the 1970s and, during that tour, several thousand Americans converted. Many of the family members of these converts complained that their love ones were manipulated by UC indoctrination. There are many cases of UC defectors sharing stories of psychological, spiritual, and labor abuse by UC leaders.

There were several important events which happened based on Moon's work in America. In 1982, he founded the *The Washington Times* newspaper. That same year he was sent to US federal prison for tax evasion. On March 23, 2004, Moon and his wife were crowned by the UC as the world's "Savior, Messiah, Returning Lord and True Parents" in the U.S. Senate building. In 2008, Moon appointed his youngest son, Hyung Jin Moon (an American citizen born in 1979), to be the new leader of the church.

In North America the UC has never had more than about ten thousand members. Nonetheless, the church exerts a level of public influence of greater proportion than its numbers would indicate. Moon's church has accumulated millions of dollars as a result of various fundraising campaigns by UC members. The church also has controlling interest in a wide ranging number of business ventures worldwide. In the education field, the UC appoints a majority of the board of trustees of the University of Bridgeport (Connecticut).

Basic Beliefs and Practice

The beliefs of the UC are a complicated mixture of Eastern philosophy, Christian and biblical terminology, and the many bizarre notions of Rev. Moon. The primary tenets are contained in several books, the most important being *The Divine Principle*.

- Rev. Moon is regarded as the "Lord of the Second Advent." He is the equivalent of Christ who has come to finish the work Jesus failed to complete.
- All reality is understood as a sort of cosmic dualism of universal polar opposites: positive/negative, active/passive, direct/indirect, objective/subjective, masculine/feminine.
- People receive the benefits of Moon's Messiahship by joining the UC, pledging obedience to him, and entering into a marriage relationship blessed by Moon.
- Members are expected to work diligently to raise money for the church and finance the Moon family's lavish lifestyle.

Essential Beliefs
God

God is the "Universal Prime Energy" who (or that) constantly interacts with the universe in the "Four Fold Foundation" of human history.

Man

God divided his creation by making Adam (masculine) and Eve (feminine) from which would come a union producing a divine bloodline of pure perfect children. Thus the God-Adam-Eve-child union would complete the four fold foundation which would thereafter be reproduced through all humanity.

Before Adam and Eve could produce perfect offspring, the serpent (symbolic for Satan) seduced Eve and produced an evil Satanic human bloodline through Cain. Later, Eve had Abel with Adam, who represents a godly line.

Salvation

Because of its corruption, God sent a redeemer to restore the human race to its proper state. Jesus was to "pay indemnity" (suffer) to redeem mankind from spiritual death and restore humanity's godly bloodline. Jesus accomplished only the first phase (spiritual redemption) of this mission. He failed in the second phase (physical redemption) because he was crucified before he could marry and produce children. Therefore, another redeemer, Rev. Moon, would come about two thousand years later to finish the divine mission.

Like Jesus, he would suffer for mankind (pay indemnity). However, he would not die violently, would live a long life, marry a perfect mate, and produce perfect children. Together they would complete the four fold foundation and form the Perfect or "True Family."

Worldview Resources

Witnessing Resource 2
Breakdown of Popular Witnessing Methods
How They Answer the Essential Questions

Every Christian witnessing methodology has been designed for the purpose of sharing the gospel message in a way that leads a person to a decision to either receive or reject Christ. There is a certain amount of diversity between the different methods, but all of them somehow explain the gospel by sharing the answer to the three essential questions from a biblical point of view (Who is God? What is a human being? What is salvation and how does one receive it?).

The purpose of this resource is to show how some of the most prominent witnessing methodologies go about sharing the gospel by answering the three questions. By seeing this spelled out, it is hoped that it will make the content of the gospel message easier for you to grasp and share.

I. Roman Road
Overview of the Methodology

The ROMAN ROAD ... is a pathway you can walk. It is a selection of Bible verses from the book of Romans in the New Testament. If you walk down this road you will end up understanding how to be saved.

1. Romans 3:23 - "For all have sinned and fall short of the glory of God."

We all have sin in our hearts. We all were born with sin. We were born under the power of sin's control. Admit that you are a sinner.

2. Romans 6:23a - "... The wages of sin is death..."

Sin has an ending. It results in death. We all face physical death, which is a result of sin. But a worse death is spiritual death that alienates us from God, and will last for all eternity. The Bible teaches that there is a place called the Lake of Fire where lost people will be in torment forever. It is the place where people who are spiritually dead will remain. Understand that you deserve death for your sin.

3. Romans 6:23b - "... But the gift of God is eternal life through Jesus Christ our Lord."

Salvation is a free gift from God to you! You can't earn this gift, but you must reach out and receive it. Ask God to forgive you and save you.

4. Romans 5:8 - "God demonstrates His own love for us, in that while we were yet sinners Christ died for us!"
When Jesus died on the cross He paid sin's penalty. He paid the price for all sin, and when He took all the sins of the world on Himself on the cross, He bought us out of slavery to sin and death! The only condition is that we believe in Him and what He has done for us, understanding that we are now joined with Him, and that He is our life. He did all this because He loved us and gave Himself for us! Give your life to God... His love poured out in Jesus on the cross is your only hope to have forgiveness and change. His love bought you out of being a slave to sin. His love is what saves you – not religion, or church membership. God loves you!

5. Romans 10:13 - "Whoever will call on the name of the Lord will be saved!"
Call out to God in the name of Jesus!

6. Romans 10:9,10 - "... If you confess with your mouth Jesus as Lord, and believe in your heart that God raised Jesus from the dead, you shall be saved; for with the heart man believes, resulting in righteousness, and with the mouth he confesses, resulting in salvation."
If you know that God is knocking on your heart's door, ask Him to come into your heart.

Jesus said in Revelation 3:20a: "Behold I stand at the door and knock, if anyone hears My voice and opens the door, I will come in to him..."

Is Jesus knocking on your heart's door?

Answers to the Essential Questions
1. Who is God?
- Romans 5:8 - God is a God of love and doesn't want us separated from him.

2. What is a human being?
- Romans 3:23 - A sinner, separated from God.
- Romans 6:23a - A being destined for eternal death unless the sin problem is satisfied.

3. What is salvation?
- Romans 6:23b - Eternal life as a free gift of God.

4. How is salvation achieved?
- Romans 10:9-13 - Believe in Jesus and call on him for salvation.
- Revelation 3:20 - Open the door of one's life.

II. Four Spiritual Laws
Overview of the Methodology
Just as there are physical laws that govern the physical universe, so are there spiritual laws which govern your relationship with God.

Law 1. God LOVES you and offers a wonderful PLAN for your life.
- God's Love - "God so loved the world that He gave His one and only Son, that whoever believes in Him shall not perish, but have eternal life." (John 3:16 NIV)
- God's Plan - [Christ speaking] "I came that they might have life, and might have it abundantly" [that it might be full and meaningful]. (John 10:10)

Why is it that most people are not experiencing the abundant life? Because...

Law 2. Man is SINFUL and SEPARATED from God. Therefore, he cannot know and experience God's love and plan for his life.
- Man Is Sinful - "All have sinned and fall short of the glory of God." (Romans 3:23)
Man was created to have fellowship with God; but, because of his stubborn self-will, he chose to go his own independent way, and fellowship with God was broken. This self-will, characterized by an attitude of active rebellion or passive indifference, is evidence of what the Bible calls sin.

- Man Is Separated - "The wages of sin is death" [spiritual separation from God]. (Romans 6:23)
  God is holy and man is sinful. A great gulf separates the two. Man is continually trying to reach God and the abundant life through his own efforts, such as a good life, philosophy, or religion - but he inevitably fails.

The third law explains the only way to bridge this gulf...

Law 3. Jesus Christ is God's ONLY provision for man's sin. Through Him you can know and experience God's love and plan for your life.
- He Died in Our Place - "God demonstrates His own love toward us, in that while we were yet sinners, Christ died for us." (Romans 5:8)
- He Rose From the Dead - "Christ died for our sins...He was buried...He was raised on the third day, according to the Scriptures...He appeared to Peter, then to the twelve. After that He appeared to more than five hundred...." (1 Corinthians 15:3-6)
- He Is the Only Way to God - "Jesus said to him, 'I am the way, and the truth, and the life; no one comes to the Father, but through Me.'" (John 14:6)

God has bridged the gulf which separates us from Him by sending His Son, Jesus Christ, to die on the cross in our place to pay the penalty for our sins.

It is not enough just to know these three laws...

Law 4. We must individually RECEIVE Jesus Christ as Savior and Lord; then we can know and experience God's love and plan for our lives.
- We Must Receive Christ - "As many as received Him, to them He gave the right to become children of God, even to those who believe in His name." (John 1:12)
- We Receive Christ Through Faith - "By grace you have been saved through faith; and that not of yourselves, it is the gift of God; not as a result of works, that no one should boast." (Ephesians 2:8,9)

- When We Receive Christ, We Experience a New Birth - (Read John 3:1-8)
- We Receive Christ by Personal Invitation - [Christ speaking] "Behold, I stand at the door and knock; if any one hears My voice and opens the door, I will come in to him." (Revelation 3:20)

Receiving Christ involves turning to God from self (repentance) and trusting Christ to come into our lives to forgive our sins and to make us what He wants us to be. Just to agree intellectually that Jesus Christ is the Son of God and that He died on the cross for your sins is not enough. Nor is it enough to have an emotional experience. You receive Jesus Christ by faith, as an act of the will.

The following explains how you can receive Christ:
- You can receive Christ right now by faith through prayer: (Prayer is talking to God) God knows your heart and is not so concerned with your words as He is with the attitude of your heart. The following is a suggested prayer: "Lord Jesus, I need You. Thank You for dying on the cross for my sins. I open the door of my life and receive You as my Savior and Lord. Thank You for forgiving my sins and giving me eternal life. Take control of the throne of my life. Make me the kind of person You want me to be."
- Does this prayer express the desire of your heart? If it does, I invite you to pray this prayer right now and Christ will come into your life, as He promised.

Answers to the Essential Questions
1. Who is God?
- God is Love - "God so loved the world that He gave His one and only Son, that whoever believes in Him shall not perish, but have eternal life." (John 3:16 NIV)
- God has a Plan - "[Christ speaking] I came that they might have life, and might have it abundantly [that it might be full and meaningful]." (John 10:10)
- God is Holy (No reference given to back up this point.)

2. What is a human being?
- Man Is Sinful - "All have sinned and fall short of the glory of God." (Romans 3:23)
- Man Is Separated from God - "The wages of sin is death [spiritual separation from God]." (Romans 6:23)

3. What is salvation?
- Salvation is bridging the gulf between a holy God and sinful man. God has bridged the gulf which separates us from Him by sending His Son, Jesus Christ, to die on the cross in our place to pay the penalty for our sins.
- Christ Died in Our Place - "God demonstrates His own love toward us, in that while we were yet sinners, Christ died for us. " (Romans 5:8)
- Christ Rose From the Dead - "Christ died for our sins...He was buried...He was raised on the third day, according to the Scriptures...He appeared to Peter, then to the twelve. After that He appeared to more than five hundred...." (1 Corinthians 15:3-6)
- Christ Is the Only Way to God - "Jesus said to him, 'I am the way, and the truth, and the life; no one comes to the Father, but through Me.'" (John 14:6)

4. How is salvation achieved?
- We Must Receive Christ - "As many as received Him, to them He gave the right to become children of God, even to those who believe in His name." (John 1:12)
- We Receive Christ Through Faith - "By grace you have been saved through faith; and that not of yourselves, it is the gift of God; not as a result of works, that no one should boast." (Ephesians 2:8,9)
- When We Receive Christ, We Experience a New Birth (Read John 3:1-8)
- We Receive Christ by Personal Invitation - [Christ speaking] "Behold, I stand at the door and knock; if any one hears My voice and opens the door, I will come in to him." (Revelation 3:20)
- The personal invitation is done through praying the "sinners prayer."

III. FAITH
Overview of the Methodology
Key Question: In your personal opinion, what do you understand it takes for a person to go to heaven?

Transition Statement: I'd like to share with you how the Bible answers this question, if it is all right. There is a word that can be used to answer this question: FAITH (spell out on fingers).

PRESENTATION
F is for FORGIVENESS. We cannot have eternal life and heaven without God's forgiveness.
"In Him [Jesus], we have redemption through His blood, the forgiveness of sins." (Ephesians 1:7a)

A is for AVAILABLE. Forgiveness is available for all. But not automatic.
"Not everyone who says to Me, "Lord, Lord," shall enter the kingdom of heaven." (Matthew 7:21a)

I is for IMPOSSIBLE. It is impossible for God to allow sin into heaven.
- God is love. "For God so loved the world that He gave His only begotten Son, that whosoever believes in Him should not perish but have everlasting life." (John 3:16)
- God is just. "For judgment is without mercy." (James 2:13a)
- Man is sinful. "For all have sinned and fall short of the glory of God." (Romans 3:23)

Question: But how can a sinful person enter heaven, where God allows no sin?

T is for TURN.
Question: If you were driving down the road and someone asked you to turn, what would s/he be asking you do to? To change direction. To turn means to repent.
- TURN from something—from sin and self.

"But unless you repent you will all likewise perish." (Luke 13:3b)
- TURN to Someone—trust Christ only.
  The Bible tells us that "Christ died for our sins according to the Scriptures; and that he was buried, and that He rose again the third day according to the Scriptures." (1 Corinthians 15:3b - 4)
  "If you confess with your mouth the Lord Jesus and believe in your heart that God has raised Him from the dead, you will be saved." (Romans 10:9)

H is for HEAVEN - Heaven is eternal life:
- Here. "I have come that they have life, and that they may have it more abundantly." (John 10:10b)
- Hereafter. "And if I go and prepare a place for you, I will come again and receive you to Myself; that where I am, there you may be also." (John 14:3)
- How? How can a person have God's forgiveness, heaven and eternal life, and Jesus as personal Savior and Lord? Explain based on leaflet picture, F.A.I.T.H. (Forsaking All I Trust Him) and Romans 10:9.

Understanding what we have shared, would you like to receive this forgiveness by trusting in Christ as your personal Savior and Lord?

Answers to the Essential Questions
1. Who is God?
- God is love - "For God so loved the world that He gave His only begotten Son, that whosoever believes in Him should not perish but have everlasting life." (John 3:16)
- God is just - "For judgment is without mercy." (James 2:13a)

2. What is a human being?
- Man is sinful - "For all have sinned and fall short of the glory of God." (Romans 3:23)

3. What is salvation?
- Salvation is eternity in relationship with God:

"I have come that they have life, and that they may have it more abundantly." (John 10:10b)

"And if I go and prepare a place for you, I will come again and receive you to Myself; that where I am, there you may be also." (John 14:3)

- But man is separated from God and must enter a relationship with him.

"Not everyone who says to Me, "Lord, Lord," shall enter the kingdom of heaven." (Matthew 7:21a)

- The relationship is restored by God's forgiveness of an individual's sin - "In Him [Jesus], we have redemption through His blood, the forgiveness of sins." (Ephesians 1:7a)
- To receive the forgiveness a person must turn from self and turn to Christ:

"But unless you repent you will all likewise perish." (Luke 13:3b)

"Christ died for our sins according to the Scriptures; and that he was buried, and that He rose again the third day according to the Scriptures." (1 Corinthians 15:3b-4)

4. How is salvation achieved?
- Salvation is achieved by confessing Christ - "If you confess with your mouth the Lord Jesus and believe in your heart that God has raised Him from the dead, you will be saved." (Romans 10:9)

IV. Steps to Peace with God
Overview of the Methodology
Step One - God's Purpose: Peace and Life
- God loves you and wants you to experience peace and life – abundant and eternal. The Bible says...
- "We have peace with God through our Lord Jesus Christ." (Romans 5:1)
- "For God so loved the world that He gave His only begotten Son, that whoever believes in Him should not perish but have everlasting life." (John 3:16)
- "I have come that they may have life, and that they may have it more abundantly." (John 10:10)

Why don't most people have this peace and abundant life that God planned for us to have?

Step Two - The Problem: Our Separation

1. God created us in His own image to have an abundant life. He did not make us as robots to automatically love and obey Him. God gave us a will and freedom of choice. We chose to disobey God and go our own willful way. We still make this choice today. This results in separation from God. The Bible says...
- "For all have sinned and fall short of the glory of God." (Romans 3:23)
- "For the wages of sin is death, but the gift of God is eternal life in Christ Jesus our Lord." (Romans 6:23)

2. Our Attempts to Reach God - People have tried in many ways to bridge this gap between themselves and God. The Bible says...
- "There is a way that seems right to a man, but in the end it leads to death." (Proverbs 14:12)
- "But your iniquities have separated you from your God; your sins have hidden his face from you, so that he will not hear." (Isaiah 59:2)

No bridge reaches God ... except one.

Step Three - God's Bridge: The Cross

Jesus Christ died on the Cross and rose from the grave. He paid the penalty for our sin and bridged the gap between God and people. The Bible says...
- "For there is one God and one mediator between God and men, the man Jesus Christ." (1 Timothy 2:5)
- "For Christ died for sins once for all, the righteous for the unrighteous, to bring you to God." (1 Peter 3:18)
- "But God demonstrates his own love for us in this: While we were still sinners, Christ died for us." (Romans 5:8)

God has provided the only way. Each person must make a choice.

Step Four - Our Response: Receive Christ

We must trust Jesus Christ as Lord and Savior and receive Him by personal invitation. The Bible says...
- "Here I am! I stand at the door and knock. If anyone hears my voice and opens the door, I will come in and eat with him, and he with me." (Revelation 3:20)
- "Yet to all who received him, to those who believed in his name, he gave the right to become children of God." (John 1:12)
- "That if you confess with your mouth, 'Jesus is Lord,' and believe in your heart that God raised Him from the dead, you will be saved." (Romans 10:9)

Where are you? Will you receive Jesus Christ right now? Here is how you can receive Christ:
1. Admit your need (I am a sinner).
2. Be willing to turn from your sins (repent).
3. Believe that Jesus Christ died for you on the Cross and rose from the grave.
4. Through prayer, invite Jesus Christ to come in and control your life through the Holy Spirit. (Receive Him as Lord and Savior.)

Answers to the Essential Questions
1. Who is God?
- God loves mankind.
  - "But God demonstrates his own love for us in this: While we were still sinners, Christ died for us." (Romans 5:8)
  - "For God so loved the world that He gave His only begotten Son, that whoever believes in Him should not perish but have everlasting life." (John 3:16)

2. What is a human being?
- Human beings are sinful and separated from God.
  - "For all have sinned and fall short of the glory of God." (Romans 3:23)
  - "For the wages of sin is death, but the gift of God is eternal life in Christ Jesus our Lord." (Romans 6:23)

Bridges: How to Share a Witness across Worldview Barriers

- "There is a way that seems right to a man, but in the end it leads to death." (Proverbs 14:12)
- "But your iniquities have separated you from your God; your sins have hidden his face from you, so that he will not hear." (Isaiah 59:2)

3. What is salvation?
   - Salvation is forgiveness of our sin so we can enter a relationship with God.
     - "For there is one God and one mediator between God and men, the man Jesus Christ." (1 Timothy 2:5)
     - "For Christ died for sins once for all, the righteous for the unrighteous, to bring you to God." (1 Peter 3:18)
     - "But God demonstrates his own love for us in this: While we were still sinners, Christ died for us." (Romans 5:8)

4. How is salvation achieved?
   - Salvation is achieved by a choice to receive God's forgiveness through Jesus Christ.
     - "Here I am! I stand at the door and knock. If anyone hears my voice and opens the door, I will come in and eat with him, and he with me." (Revelation 3:20)
     - "Yet to all who received him, to those who believed in his name, he gave the right to become children of God." (John 1:12)
     - "That if you confess with your mouth, 'Jesus is Lord,' and believe in your heart that God raised Him from the dead, you will be saved." (Romans 10:9)

V. Evangelism Explosion
Overview of the Methodology
May I ask you a question?
Q #1 – Have you come to the place in your spiritual life where you know for certain that if you were to die today that you would go to heaven? 1 John 5:13 (You can know you have eternal life.)

Let me ask you a second question...

Q #2 - Suppose you were to die today and stand before God and He were to say to you, "why should I let you into My heaven? What would you say?

The Gospel Message
A. Grace
    1. Heaven is a free gift. - "For the wages of sin is death, but the gift of God is eternal life in Christ Jesus our Lord." (Romans 6:23)
    2. It is not earned or deserved. - "For it is by grace you have been saved, through faith — and this not from yourselves, it is the gift of God - not by works, so that no one can boast." (Ephesians 2:8-9)

B. Man
    1. Is a sinner. - "For all have sinned and fall short of the glory of God." (Romans 3:23)
        Sin defined. - "Be perfect, therefore, as your heavenly Father is perfect." (Matthew 5:48)
    2. Cannot save himself. - "There is a way that seems right to a man, but in the end it leads to death." (Proverbs 14:12)

C. God
    1. God is merciful - therefore doesn't want punish us. (1 John 4:8b)
    2. God is just - therefore must punish us. - "Yet he does not leave the guilty unpunished; he punishes the children and their children for the sin of the fathers to the third and fourth generation." (Exodus 34:7b)

God solved this problem in the Person of Jesus Christ.

D. Christ.
    1. Who He is – the infinite God-man:
- "In the beginning was the Word, and the Word was with God, and the Word was God." (John 1:1)
- "The Word became flesh and made his dwelling among us. We have seen his glory, the glory of the One and Only, who came from the Father, full of grace and truth.

- "Thomas said to him, 'My Lord and my God!'" (John 20:28)

2. What He did – He died on the cross and rose from the dead to pay the penalty for our sins and to purchase a place in heaven for us which He offers as a gift.

E. Faith - Key to heaven
   1. What it is not – mere intellectual assent.
      - "You believe that there is one God. Good! Even the demons believe that — and shudder." (James 2:19)
      - "'What do you want with us, Son of God?' they shouted. 'Have you come here to torture us before the appointed time?'" (Matthew 8:29)
   2. What it is – trusting in Jesus Christ alone for eternal life.
      - "They replied, 'Believe in the Lord Jesus, and you will be saved — you and your household.'" (Acts 16:31)

Answers to the Essential Questions

1. Who is God?
   - God is merciful – therefore doesn't want punish us. (1 John 4:8b)
   - God is just – therefore must punish us. - "Yet he does not leave the guilty unpunished; he punishes the children and their children for the sin of the fathers to the third and fourth generation." (Exodus 34:7b)
   - He became Jesus – the infinite God-man. - "In the beginning was the Word, and the Word was with God, and the Word was God." (John 1:1)
   "The Word became flesh and made his dwelling among us. We have seen his glory, the glory of the One and Only, who came from the Father, full of grace and truth." (John 1:14)

2. What is a human being?
   - 1. Is a sinner. - "For all have sinned and fall short of the glory of God." (Romans 3:23)

3. What is salvation?
    - Heaven is a free gift. - "For the wages of sin is death, but the gift of God is eternal life in Christ Jesus our Lord." (Romans 6:23)
    - It is not earned or deserved. - "For it is by grace you have been saved, through faith — and this not from yourselves, it is the gift of God – not by works, so that no one can boast." (Ephesians 2:8-9)
    - What it is not – mere intellectual assent. - "You believe that there is one God. Good! Even the demons believe that — and shudder." (James 2:19)

    "'What do you want with us, Son of God?' they shouted. 'Have you come here to torture us before the appointed time?'" (Matthew 8:29)

4. How is salvation achieved?
    - Man cannot save himself. - "There is a way that seems right to a man, but in the end it leads to death." (Proverbs 14:12)
    - A person must trust in Jesus Christ alone for eternal life. - "They replied, 'Believe in the Lord Jesus, and you will be saved — you and your household.'" (Acts 16:31)

Witnessing Resource 3
The Seven Worldview Questions

Identifying the basic fundamental questions of a worldview or a particular belief system is as simple as answering the seven worldview questions. The answers can then be compared to the definitions of the various worldviews to identify which one you are dealing with. The seven worldview questions are:

1. What is the nature of ultimate reality? (God)
2. What is the nature of material reality? (Material Universe)
3. What is a human being? (Mankind)
4. What happens to a person at death? (Afterlife)
5. Why is it possible to know anything at all? (Knowledge)
6. How do we know right and wrong? (Morality)
7. What is the meaning of human history? (Purpose)

This book takes a simplified approach to get at the worldview questions. We have compressed the seven questions into what we have identified as the "essentials." For our purposes, the seven worldview questions above compress into the "essentials" as follows:

1. Who is God?
   What is the nature of ultimate reality?
   How do we know right and wrong?
   What is the meaning of human history?

2. What is a human being?
   What is a human being?
   Why is it possible to know anything at all?

3. What is salvation and how does one achieve it?
   What is the nature of material reality?
   What happens to a person at death?

Witnessing Resource 4
Witnessing Issues Related to Cross Cultural Missions

Professional missionaries have almost always had to have a larger skill set in order to share their faith than the average lay person. The reason for this is that they typically have to deal with people whose lifestyle, values, norms and beliefs are radically different than their own. They must become proficient at building a bridge across these differences.

In our current day, there are so many more opportunities for the non-professional to also have these opportunities. As such, it is important for those who do short-term missions and wish to share Christ to also learn these skills. Below is an outline of some of the specific things that need to be learned.

1. Learn as much as you can about the background and culture of the group you are attempting to reach.
- Learn as much as possible about the history of the society.
- Learn the cultural expectations and taboos of the society.
- Discern the way those in the society are most willing and/or able to learn new information.
- Discover who the cultural gatekeepers are and how you can make friends with them.
- Discover the best ways to gain acceptance in order to interact with the populace.
- If there are language issues, figure out how to get around those.

2. Map the religious heritage of the group you are trying to reach.
- Map how they answer the essential belief questions (their worldview beliefs).
- Map the entire religion.
  - Learn the name of the religion.
  - Learn what God/gods/philosophy they believe in and as much specific information as you can find about Him/them/it.
  - Learn the ritual practices of the belief and why each is important.
  - Learn the history of the belief.

- Learn any mythology which goes along with the belief.
  - Learn the doctrines (related to essential and non-essential beliefs) of the faith.
  - Learn the belief's hierarchical leadership structure and the roles of the leaders.
  - Learn what the belief teaches about the consequences of not following the belief.
  - Learn how the average believer interacts with the religion.
  - Learn what the belief teaches about origins.
  - Learn what the belief teaches about the afterlife.
  - Learn what the belief teaches about morality.
- Learn what the belief teaches about the meaning of human life.

Discussion and Leader's Guides

Bridges
Small Group Discussion Guide

This book can be used as the basis for small group study. Use the questions associated with each chapter to facilitate discussion for each class session.

Chapter 1 - Starting with the Basics
Discussion Questions
1. What, specifically, must happen for an encounter legitimately to be called a Christian witness?
2. What is the role God plays in the witnessing process?
3. How does God fulfill his part?
4. What role does the Christian play in the witnessing process?
5. Name as many ways as you can think of as to how Christians can fulfill their role in the witnessing process.
6. What role does the one being witnessed to play in the witnessing process?
7. What possible ways can the person being witnessed to respond?
8. What are the possible ways the Christian can address those responses?

Chapter 2 - Why a Knowledge of Worldview is Important for Witness
Discussion Questions
1. What is a worldview?
2. What is it about worldview that makes it so difficult to grasp?
3. What is it about worldview that makes it so difficult to communicate across worldview barriers?
4. In general terms, why is an understanding of worldview important in the witnessing process?
5. How does an understanding of worldview help us understand faith?
6. How does an understanding of worldview help us understand that the gospel is objective truth?
7. How does an understanding of worldview help us have confidence in the truth of the gospel?
8. How does an understanding of worldview help us understand other people's beliefs?

9. How does an understanding of worldview help us understand the weaknesses of non-biblical beliefs?

Chapter 3 - Overview of the Witnessing Process
Discussion Questions
1. What kind of due diligence does a Christian need to do in order to become an effective witness?
2. What four specific knowledge components are important for becoming an effective witness and what is the content of each?
3. What two specific personal components are important for becoming an effective witness and what is the content of each?
4. What is the importance of relationships in the witnessing process and how should they be handled?
5. How can a Christian go about learning another person's worldview?
6. What, specifically, needs to be understood to map another person's worldview?
7. Why is it important to understand the commitment level of the one you wish to witness to?

Chapter 4 - The Starting Point for Witness
Discussion Questions
1. Why is it important to build a "worldview bridge" before building a "gospel bridge?"
2. What is Naturalism?
3. What is the starting point of witness to a Naturalist?
4. What is an Animist?
5. What is the starting point of witness to an Animist?
6. What is a Far Eastern Thought believer?
7. What is the starting point of witness to a Far Eastern Thought believer?
8. What is a Theist?
9. What is the starting point of witness to a Theist?
10. What is a hybrid believer?
11. What is the starting point of witness to a hybrid believer?

Chapter 5 - The Art of Argument
Discussion Questions
1. What does it mean to argue on the offensive?

Bridges: How to Share a Witness across Worldview Barriers

2. What are some ways non-believers try to put Christians on the defensive?
3. What are the weaknesses of Naturalism?
4. What are the weaknesses of Animism?
5. What are the weaknesses of Far Eastern Thought?
6. What are the weaknesses of non-Christian Theism?
7. What are the weaknesses of hybrid belief systems?
8. When is it appropriate to argue defensively?
9. What are the major points of argument to defend the Christian faith?

Chapter 6 - Sharing an Effective Witness Presentation
Discussion Questions
1. What is necessary to get people into your witnessing presentation?
2. What is necessary to distinguish non-Christian beliefs from Christian faith?
3. Give an explanation of the five parts of the scope of the Christian worldview.
4. What comprises the content of the gospel message?
5. At what point is it appropriate to ask for a decision and how should we decide when one has reached that point?
6. What is the appropriate follow through with a person when you actually share the gospel?

Chapter 7 - Witnessing in Daily Life
Discussion Questions
1. What is the difference between sharing the gospel by means of words or by one's lifestyle?
2. Is it appropriate to pick one over the other? Why or why not? If so, what makes the difference?
3. Under what circumstances is cold call witnessing a good thing?
4. Under what circumstances is cold call witnessing not necessarily a good thing?
5. How can common relationships be a platform for sharing a witness?
6. What factors determine who should go on mission trips to share a witness and how does one know when it is appropriate?

Bridges
Witness Training Guide

This book can be used as a tool for training in effective witness. Some of the training involves simply becoming familiar with a particular knowledge base. Other parts involve mastery of particular pieces of knowledge or skills. You may use the activities listed under each chapter below as a checklist of the things you should become familiar with and master from this book.

Chapter 1 - Starting with the Basics
Training Activities
1. Master the definition of a witness. (noun and verb)
2. Become familiar with the three participants in the witnessing process and their appropriate functions.

Chapter 2 - Why a Knowledge of Worldview is Important for Witness
Training Activities
1. Master the definition of a worldview.
2. Become familiar with the origins of an individual's worldview.
3. Become familiar with the four issues which make changing worldviews difficult.
4. Become familiar with the five reasons worldview is important in the witnessing process.

Chapter 3 - Overview of the Witnessing Process
Training Activities
1. Become familiar with the four areas of knowledge that a Christian witness needs to grasp.
2. Become familiar with the three personal issues a Christian witness needs to incorporate into his or her life.
3. Become familiar with the importance of relationships in the witnessing process.
4. Become familiar with the need to gather an individual's worldview information for effective witness.
5. Master the three necessary components for analyzing and mapping an individual's worldview foundation.

6. Understand the importance of an individual's commitment level for effective witness.

Chapter 4 - The Starting Point for Witness
Training Activities
1. Become familiar with the two bridges for effective witness and how they differ.
2. Master an overall understanding of Naturalism (basic assumption, belief systems, answers to the essential questions, starting point for witness).
3. Master an overall understanding of Animism (basic assumption, belief systems, answers to the essential questions, starting point for witness).
4. Master an overall understanding of Far Eastern Thought (basic assumption, belief systems, answers to the essential questions, starting point for witness).
5. Master an overall understanding of non-Christian Theism (basic assumption, belief systems, answers to the essential questions, starting point for witness)
6. Master an overall understanding of hybrid belief systems (basic assumption, belief systems, answers to the essential questions, starting point for witness).

Chapter 5 - The Art of Argument
Training Activities
1. Become familiar with the concept of arguing "offensively."
   - What does arguing offensively mean?
   - What is important about relationships in the process of arguing?
   - What tactics do people use to put Christians on the defensive?
2. Master the specific problem areas of non-Christian worldview positions (Naturalism, Animism, Far Eastern Thought, non-Christian Theism, Hybrid belief systems).
3. Become familiar with the four areas that Christian witnesses must master to effectively argue with those from other worldview platforms.
4. Become familiar with the concept of arguing "defensively" and when it is appropriate to operate from that position.
5. Master the primary categories for defending the Christian faith.

Chapter 6 - Sharing an Effective Witness Presentation
Training Activities
1. Master the means by which we get people into a gospel presentation situation.
2. Master the ability to compare and contrast other belief systems to the Christian faith.
3. Master the five elements of the scope of the Christian worldview to the point you can easily share it with non-believers.
4. Master the content of the Christian gospel message.
5. Master the ability to appropriately bring a person to a decision to receive Christ.
6. Master the ability to follow-up with those you witness to – regardless of their decision.

Chapter 7 - Witnessing in Daily Life
Training Activities
1. Become familiar with the possible contexts for sharing a witness.